Late Than ...,

DAILY
MEDITATIONS

Front cover: © igoriss/iStock

Prosveta S.A – 83600 Fréjus (France)

ISBN 978-2-8184-0531-4

original edition: 978-2-8184-0530-7

digital edition : 978-2-8184-0595-6

Omraam Mikhaël Aïvanhov

DAILY MEDITATIONS

2023

PROSVETA

Foreword

Every morning, before you do anything else, you must give yourself a few quiet moments of reflection so as to begin your day in peace and harmony, and unite yourself to the Creator by dedicating the new day to Him through prayer, meditation.

It is the beginning that is all-important, for it is then, at the beginning, that new forces are set in motion and given direction. If we want to act wisely and well, we have to begin by casting some light on the situation. You do not look for something or start work in the dark; you start by lighting a lamp so that you can see what you are doing. And you can apply the same principle to every area in life: in order to know what to do and how to do it, you have to switch on the light – in other words, to concentrate and look into yourself. Without this light you will wander in all directions and knock on many different doors, and you will never achieve anything worthwhile.

Our days follow the direction that we give to our first thoughts in the morning, for, depending on whether we are mindful or not, we either clear the way ahead or litter it with all kinds of useless and even dangerous debris. Disciples of initiatic science know how to begin the day so that it may be fruitful and rich in God's grace, and so that they may share that grace with those around them. They understand how important it is to begin the day with

5

one fundamental thought around which all the other thoughts of the day may revolve.

If you keep your sights fixed on a definite goal, a clear orientation, an ideal, all your activities will gradually organize themselves and fall into line in such a way as to contribute to the realization of that ideal. Even the negative or alien thoughts or feelings that attempt to infiltrate you will be deflected and put at the service of the divine world. Yes, even they will be forced to follow the direction you have chosen. In this way, thanks to the fundamental thought that you place in your head and your heart first thing in the morning, your whole day will be recorded in the book of life.

And, since everything we do is recorded, once you have lived one glorious day, one day of eternal life, not only will that day be recorded, not only will it never die, but it will endeavor to get the days that follow to imitate it. Try to live just one day as well as you possibly can, therefore, and it will influence all your days: it will persuade them to listen to its testimony and follow its example, so as to be well balanced, orderly, and harmonious.

Omraam Mikhaël Aïvanhov

Between 1938 and 1985, Omraam Mikhaël Aïvanhov elaborated a spiritual teaching in almost five thousand improvised talks. His words have been preserved in their entirety, as the talks given between 1938 and the early 1960s were taken down in shorthand, and the later ones were recorded on tape and latterly on video.

Many of these recordings have been published in book form by Prosveta, providing a comprehensive guide to the teaching.

GLOSSARY

Definitions of terms as used by the Master Omraam Mikhaël Aïvanhov:

Brotherhood: a collectivity governed by a truly cohesive spirit, in which each individual works consciously for the good of all. (Daily Meditations 2007: 24 February) A brotherhood is a collectivity whose members share the common bond of a broad, luminous consciousness and work with and for each other, and more than that, they work for the whole world. True brotherhood is universal.

Caduceus: the two snakes represent the two currents, positive and negative, of astral light known traditionally as Od and Ob. The one is luminous and hot, the other is dark and cold; one is white, the other black. (Izvor 237 ch. 9)

Collectivity [human]: a group of people, usually quite extensive, united by a common interest, a common organization or common sentiments, or living in the same place or country. (Prosveta, France, provided it)

Collectivity [cosmic]: the totality of beings in the universe, both visible and invisible.

Disinterestedness: refers not to a lack of interest but to an altruism, an absence of bias motivated by interest or advantage. This is a central part of the Master's philosophy. (A New Dawn, part 2, p.120)

Entities: disincarnate beings, drawn to humans and to nature. They may be either light or dark beings, depending on the quality of the vibrations of the person or place attracting them.

Higher Self, Lower Self: must be understood within the context of the Master's teaching concerning the two natures in human beings, the human lower self and the divine higher self, which he calls respectively personality and individuality. (Love and Sexuality, part 2, p. 42)

Impersonal: refers not to a coldness of attitude but to the absence of referral to self.

Individuality: see 'higher self, lower self'.

Personality: see 'higher self, lower self'.

Psychic: (adjective – as in 'psychic life / world / bodies, etc.'): refers not to mediumship but to a human being's subtle energy beyond the physical, i.e. heart and mind (and soul, or soul and spirit, according to the context).

The Rock: a platform at the top of a hill near the Bonfin, where the Master and his disciples gathered every morning, in spring and summer, to meditate and watch the sun rise.

1 January

The New Year* is completely fresh and new, but at the same time it is already worn out, because the human beings who greet it are mired in their same miserable thoughts, feelings and habits. They have not thought to wash out their vessels before filling them with the pure waters of the new year. Yet this is the first thing we learn in the kitchen: we wash a dirty saucepan before filling it with clean water. But when it comes to filling their hearts and souls and minds with something pure, people never think of cleansing themselves first. They forget that the rules that apply in the kitchen also apply to their inner lives!

If you want the new year to be truly new for you, think of it as someone very rich who is coming to visit you bearing marvellous gifts. Prepare many places within yourselves to receive those gifts, clean them tirelessly so as to clear out the old clutter from your hearts and minds. You must have a place ready and waiting inside yourselves before the new year arrives.

---

* Related reading: *The New Year,* Brochure No. 301.

2 January

*S*o many people have come to me and said, 'Why did I find your teaching so late in life? I have spent my whole life in doubt and error, and now not only is it too late to undo my mistakes, but it is too late to really start a new life.' It is true that it is better to find the light when we are young so that we may guide our life by it, but that does not mean that it is too late now that you are old. Even if you have very little time left to live, you can still learn the essential truths and immerse yourself in them. In this way, you will attain a higher level of consciousness before leaving this world.

This is the great difference between the physical and the spiritual life: if you have never learned to play a musical instrument, pilot a helicopter or even sew or knit, you cannot expect to do so when you are eighty.* But when it comes to learning the laws that govern the world of the soul and the spirit, it is never too late. Every effort you make in this direction will not only make it easier for you to enter the light of the next world, but it will also help you to prepare for your next incarnation.

* Related reading: *Light is a Living Spirit,* Izvor No. 212, Chap. 8.

Christ said, *'No one comes to the Father except through me.'* This means that humans can truly be in communion with God only through their higher soul, for Christ is the Son of God who is present within each human being as a hidden spark. When you are in communion with your higher soul, you are communing with the Christ within,* and through him with God. You can go to God only through your higher soul because this is the purest dimension of your being. This is why you must never abandon the practice of meditation, for it is by meditation that you free yourself from the physical plane and rise to the Godhead, the living principle of your higher soul.

* Related reading: *Sons and Daughters of God,* Izvor No. 240, Chap. 7.

4 January

We have to struggle against the weight and obscurity of our own being every day. Yes, each and every day. You might say, 'How long will this last?' As long as human beings reincarnate on earth, they must take on a physical body, and a physical body is by its very nature heavy and coarse because it has to abide by the laws of matter. As soon as their evolution is complete,* the bonds that tie human beings to the earth are severed and they are freed from this crushing weight and darkness. But it is no good deluding yourselves; as long as you are on earth there is no escape. However, those who are conscious and truly spiritual never give up the struggle; they cling to the Lord, to light and love, to hope and faith, and by means of prayer and meditation free themselves more and more often from the burden of physical matter.

* Related reading: *The Laughter of a Sage,* Izvor No. 243, Chap. 8.

5 January

*H*uman beings are like lumps of cold, grey iron. Only contact with fire, spiritual fire, can transform them. Physical fire has the power to make iron malleable so that a blacksmith can give it a new shape. In the same way, the spiritual fire* of divine love can plunge a person into a spiritual state wherein they rid themselves of their old, drab, ungainly form and receive a new, luminous, radiant one. This is something that true mystics and initiates have always known. They have learned to find the true fire that burns within their soul and spirit and to plunge themselves into it so as to become completely malleable. Then, by means of a work with thought, they pound and hammer out new forms for themselves.

* Related reading: *The Living Book of Nature,* Izvor No. 216, Chap. 6.

6 January

*E*very now and then you say, 'I had a splendid idea today', without realizing that your idea was a spiritual being that came to visit you. An idea is not a purely mental process; it is a living entity that manifests itself through you. And if, instead of treasuring this divine idea* and putting yourself at its service, you start worrying about what your wife or children or neighbours will say, you drive away that luminous being, and in so doing you impoverish yourself. So be careful, and from now on, when a luminous idea comes to you, clean and purify everything so that it may stay and create abundance and beauty within you.

* Related reading: *Harmony and Health,* Izvor No. 225, Chap. 3.

7 January

Learn to attune yourselves with the spiritual forces and entities that fill the infinite reaches of the universe, for in this way you will receive the blessings that belong to perfect life: light, joy, peace and love. When you have learned to be in harmony with the universe, your vibrations will be so intense that all those you meet will be swept along in your wake. You will be a beneficent force, bearing with you the gifts of heaven. The only way to do good and bring light to others is through your own harmonious life,* and you must prepare yourselves for this by making harmony your ideal.

* Related reading: *Harmony and Health,* Izvor No. 225, Chap. 2 and 3.

8 January

Rise to greater and greater heights – you have the right to do so and no one can stop you. In fact, this is the only absolute right that God has given to all his creatures. Each time you take a step upwards, that is to say, each time you succeed in resisting a temptation, in conquering or even transforming a weakness or a vice, orders automatically go out from heaven: an entity is sent to help you, you are given certain powers, your circumstances begin to change. But it is not your business to see that these things happen. The only thing you have to do is to overcome obstacles and difficulties by rising above them.* All the rest will be given to you automatically.

* Related reading: *Toward a Solar Civilization,* Izvor No. 201, Chap. 3.

9 January

In their prayers and meditations, disciples must always begin by turning to the saints, prophets, initiates and great masters, for it is they who have the mission to look after human beings. Then, they can rise to a higher plane and invoke the angels, for of all the celestial hierarchies, it is the angels who are closest to human beings; it is they who hear their prayers and give them the help they ask for. Only then should they try to invoke the archangels. As for the principalities and the more exalted ranks of the angelic hosts, it is useless to try and make yourself heard by them. There are countless worlds in the infinite reaches of space, filled with billions of creatures, and these exalted hierarchies have immense tasks to fulfil at great distances from the earth; they have very little contact with our planet.

Those who have been given the mission of taking care of humanity are mainly beings who once lived on earth and, having left it, still remember it. They are still attached to this world; they still have promises to keep. Disciples must know about the heavenly hierarchies*, but if they want their prayers to be answered, they must address them to those who are nearest.

* Related reading: *Angels and other Mysteries of the Tree of Life,* Izvor No. 236, Chap. 1 and 3.

10 January

Life* is a long voyage of discovery in the course of which we explore unknown regions of the world and, above all, the unknown regions of our own inner world. Some of the regions we visit are hospitable and we can linger in them at least for a while. Others are hostile and we must avoid them, or, if we have the misfortune to set foot in them, we must flee from them as quickly as possible.

Poets and philosophers often speak of life as a journey, for even if you spend your entire life at home in the same room, you can find within yourself every phenomenon of nature and every variety of landscape that the world has to offer. There are days when you complain, 'I don't know what the matter is, I feel stifled'. Well, this is because, without realizing it, you have descended too far into the subterranean regions and the atmosphere is weighing you down. The answer is to rise to a higher level and get out into the fresh air. And if you sometimes feel buoyant and inspired, as though the laws of gravity had lost their hold on you, it is because, consciously or unconsciously, you have succeeded in scaling an inner mountain.

* Related reading: *The Seeds of Happiness,* Izvor No. 231, Chap. 11.

11 January

Only the Absolute, God Himself, can fulfil you, and it is only if you persevere in your quest for God that you can obtain all that you desire – and more besides. The great thing is to understand the nature of what you are doing and never to be discouraged. Anyone who reflects on the nature of their activity knows that certain difficulties are occupational hazards that come with the job.* But this does not prevent them from persevering for they know that every occupation has its drawbacks.

Why should people who have chosen the spiritual life not experience occupational hazards like everybody else? If they give way to discouragement and abandon their chosen path, it shows that they have not understood this; if they had, their difficulties would stimulate them to continue with even greater ardour. When you are discouraged, your very discouragement should be a reason to renew your courage. This is true alchemy, the true philosopher's stone.

* Related reading: *The Powers of Thought,* Izvor No. 224, Chap. 13.

12 January

The Universal White Brotherhood* is not a new religion; it is the religion of Christ presented in a new form adapted to our times. All those who decide to work with the eternal, changeless principles of Christ belong to the Universal White Brotherhood. They are not destroying anything, they are not working against Christ; they are not introducing a new religion. They are simply discarding certain forms which, in the course of centuries, have become meaningless.

If someone clings to forms it means that they have not understood the underlying principles and, imagining that their salvation lies in the form, they sleep soundly under its protection. Yes, those who trust in forms fall asleep. If you want to evolve, you must work with principles and rely less on forms. The Gospels tell us that, *'the letter kills but the Spirit gives life'*. Those who cling to the letter, to forms, claim to be motivated by the love of God; but it is not their love of God, it is their sloth that makes them refuse to be animated and led by the life-giving spirit that ceaselessly renews all forms.

* Related reading: *A Philosophy of Universality,* Izvor No. 206.

13 January

Let light be your inner yardstick. Sometimes when you are meditating or in a very spiritual state of mind, you can sense that your whole being becomes luminous, as though a myriad lamps or the sun itself were shining within you. Sometimes you can even feel this light shining out from your face. When you rise to the higher levels of kindness and generosity, gentleness and purity, everything within becomes brighter* and you are filled with light; and this light can actually be seen. But when you harbour feelings of jealousy, egoism and greed, you do not need to look in the mirror to know that your face reflects darkness; you can feel it physically.

* Related reading: *Light is a Living Spirit,* Izvor No. 212, Chap. 5.

14 January

Our vocal chords are a musical instrument unlike any other, for they are not external to us; all that we experience in life and all the thoughts and emotions of our minds and hearts are reflected in them. This is why those who want to cultivate their voice and ensure that its beauty endures must not only take care of their health, they must also watch over the states of their inner life.

The voice of a singer who leads a pure, well-balanced, harmonious life becomes stronger and increases in volume, flexibility, smoothness, subtlety and range; and as it obeys them more and more readily,* they are able to convey what they wish to express more easily. Instead of serving only their personal whims and passions, instead of seeking only pleasure or financial gain, singers should pursue a high ideal, for in this way they ally themselves with the spiritual entities who can help and guide them and show them ever better ways of improving and refining their voice.

* Related reading: *Creation: Artistic and Spiritual,* Izvor No. 223, Chap. 5.

15 January

Most people are inclined to believe that every idea that pops into their mind is necessarily sound, and this attitude gives rise to all misunderstandings. As long as they have not worked to purify themselves and vibrate in harmony with the world of love, light and truth, their antennae will be subject to error and the messages they pick up will be distorted and biased.

You must stop clinging to an idea for no better reason than that it has occurred to you. Every sensation or idea, as well as the nature and origin of all your motivations, must be carefully scrutinized. If you are sincere, you will have to admit that most of your convictions or impulses generally come from below. The trouble is that if you have no standard by which to judge, you will fail to recognize where they stem from and hasten to follow their dictates. And this is the cause of all conflicts and dissensions: everyone is ignorant, no one has any discernment, and no one bothers to verify the validity of their opinions and assertions. A disciple's first concern must be to acquire criteria so as to verify the basis and origin of the motive behind their every action.*

* Related reading: *Looking into the Invisible,* Izvor No. 228, Chap. 2.

16 January

Novices in the spiritual life often plunge
headlong into schemes that are too ambitious,
and this inevitably leads to accidents or disillusionment. If at your first attempt you try to
jump a chasm that is too wide, you will fall
in and by the time you climb out – supposing
you ever manage to do so – you will have had
such a shock that you might refuse to undertake
anything else, however modest. But if you start
by jumping only one or two feet and increase this
day by day, you will gradually gain confidence
and end by clearing an immense width. The
same thing applies in the spiritual life.

I have already given you so many methods
– a few words to say, a simple gesture to make –
but you do not use these methods, they seem too
paltry. And yet it is precisely simple methods
such as these that can prepare you for great
achievements,* whereas spectacular beginnings
only end in disaster. In their desire to become
clairvoyant or to obtain other psychic powers
without delay, many people start dabbling in
occult practices and the consequences are
disastrous!

* Related reading: *The Book of Divine Magic,* Izvor No. 226,
Chap. 16.

17 January

Strive to imbue your love with purity and light, for this is the only way to be sure that those you love flourish and fulfil themselves. True love bestows every blessing: joy, peace, beauty, and health. Above all, it gives meaning to life.* If you see those you love wasting away, you must question your feelings and ask yourself, 'What have I done to harm this creature? I was supposed to be tending to them, just as a gardener cares for their flowers, but I have only made them wilt.' You have nothing to be proud of, on the contrary, it is time you started looking for ways to correct your mistakes. Your love should help those you love to grow, and it is only when you see this happening that you have a right to feel proud and happy, and grateful to heaven.

* Related reading: *Light is a Living Spirit,* Izvor No. 212, Chap. 5.

18 January

Prayer* is the breathing of the soul, and this breathing affects not only our psychic bodies but our physical body as well. Sincere, ardent prayer triggers a succession of reactions that can even modify the movement of electrons in the very substance of our physical body. The nature of the faculty by means of which a person strives to reach a Being or a world of a higher order is still not understood.

Let us say, for example, that you are praying for light, love, peace or even health; the sincerity and fervour of your prayer raise you inwardly to another plane. You say that you are praying to God. No doubt; but God, who exists outside of you, of course, also exists within you, and it is to this higher power within that you pray. And when you touch this inner power through prayer, it responds with a gift, the gift of pure, intense currents of life, which flow through you and illuminate and harmonize everything they touch. So the pattern found in breathing is found also in prayer: there is the upward movement (inhaling) as you make your request, followed by the downward movement (exhaling) as your prayer is answered with blessings from above.

* Related reading: *The True Meaning of Christ's Teaching,* Izvor No. 215, Chap. 1.

19 January

When you experience great joy do not drink it to the dregs all at once; always keep a few drops in reserve, otherwise you will soon lose it again. Rejoice, but within limits. If you ignore this rule this is what will happen: you will be like a drunkard who, having had one too many, staggers drunkenly along the street, colliding first with one wall, reeling back and then colliding with the other, as if the walls were bouncing him from side to side. In all things, even in joy, moderation is desirable and there are precautions to be taken, for our inner life is also governed by the laws of equilibrium. So try not to go to extremes, otherwise one extreme will simply send you back to the opposite extreme and you will be forever tossed back and forth between states over which you have no control.

20 January

Most people only have to hear the words 'renunciation' or 'sacrifice' to be seized with terror. They say, 'If I have to renounce this or that I shall die!' And it is quite true, they will die if they fail to understand that the whole purpose of renunciation* is to obtain something even better. Nature has planned it all perfectly: we eat, drink and breathe, and no one wants us to deny these needs; we simply have to refine them and transpose them from the lower planes onto a higher plane.

So stop thinking that privation means death. On the contrary, privation can lead to a more subtle life. To give up something is to enrich oneself by transforming one kind of energy into energy of a subtler kind. Nature gives us countless examples of this phenomenon, and if we fail to understand how it applies on the spiritual level, we shall continue to stagnate. It is this stagnation that leads to death.

* Related reading: *Man's Two Natures: Human and Divine*, Izvor No. 213, Chap. 6.

21 January

Depending on the way a human being lives and behaves, their vibrations will be tuned to the wavelength of certain entities, and it is this attunement that attracts those entities. This is the most powerful secret of magic, and it has been known from the earliest ages of man. In ancient Egypt, for instance, the initiates concentrated, recited set formulas and put on certain vestments or masks so as to identify with the gods Osiris or Horus. By vibrating on the exact same wavelength* as the god, for a brief moment they became an incarnation of this sublime entity, thus enabling him to speak and manifest himself through them.

We can create a bond between ourselves and something or someone else only by tuning in to the same vibrational frequency. This is the law of physics on which radio is based, and Initiates were familiar with it long before contemporary physicists. Also, since they understood it more perfectly, they knew that it applied on the psychic, spiritual plane as well as on the physical plane. This is why they gave their disciples rules and methods designed to help them to vibrate in unison with heavenly entities, receive their messages and benefit from their virtues.

* Related reading: *What is a Spiritual Master?*, Izvor No. 207, Chap. 8 and 11.

22 January

In both work and play, human beings spend their energies without heed, and while they are busy acquiring a few trinkets or enjoying some little pleasures here and there, their life drains away because they are not mindful of it. Many people think that the mere fact of being alive entitles them to use their life to indulge all their appetites, amass as much wealth as possible, and show off to everyone else. They draw without restraint on their vital reserves and then, when there is nothing left, they are obliged to abandon all their activities abruptly. How senseless to squander life in this way, for when it is all gone you are left with nothing!

Wise men have always considered life to be the one essential.* They tell us to treasure it, to purify and sanctify it and to eliminate whatever impairs or weakens it, because it is thanks to life that we can obtain everything our soul and spirit desire: intelligence, strength, beauty, power... everything.

* Related reading: *Youth: Creators of the Future,* Izvor No. 233, Chap. 7 and 17.

23 January

*A*ll those who do not work for the kingdom of God will always be hungry, thirsty, vulnerable and careworn. Why? Because they receive no wages, symbolically speaking. But those who serve heaven and work for the kingdom of God receive a marvellous salary every day and every hour in the form of strength, currents of light and love, joy, delight and wonder. When you meet such people, you cannot help but be struck by their joy, and if you ask them why they are so joyful, they will say, 'It is because we work in the vineyards of the Lord. This is our reward.'*

* Related reading: *The Seeds of Happiness,* Izvor No. 231, Chap. 6.

24 January

When material conditions are ideal, our will does not have much opportunity to exert itself. It is when things are difficult and we are in need that we are obliged to exercise our will. All those who have stood out by reason of their exceptional character have always been beset by difficulties, privations, and even persecution in their lives. I am not saying this in order to encourage you to go out and look for poverty, illness or persecution. I simply want you to understand that the conditions you should seek are those that allow you to exercise your willpower and make progress on your upward path toward the divine world.*

* Related reading: *The Philosopher's Stone in the Gospels and in Alchemy,* Izvor No. 241, Chap. 1.

25 January

In wanting to possess things, we are exercising a right that nature herself has given us. Our physical bodies, for instance, belong to us and we are well advised to keep them for ourselves. We may of course give away something of ourselves – our words, looks or smiles – but we must not give away our bodies. Look at a tree: it keeps possession of its roots, trunk and branches, but it gives away its fruit.

This is in accordance with the designs of nature,* and Initiates, who understand the lesson of nature, do exactly what a tree does: they keep their roots, trunk and branches, symbolically speaking, but they give away their fruit, that is to say, their thoughts and feelings, their words, their light and their strength. You too must learn what to give away and what to keep for yourselves.

* Related reading: *Man, Master of his Destiny,* Izvor No. 202, Chap. 8.

26 January

*T*hrough prayer and silent meditation you accumulate energy and then, when you speak, your words are meaningful, vibrant and dynamic because they are filled with love, light and divine power. This love and light, this divine power is the Word, the Logos, and it is this that gives your words their potency.* The first step is to think and feel; this is the Word. Secondly, you look for a form in which to express your thoughts, and this is speech, the words you choose in a specific language that make your thoughts accessible to other human beings. But the Word itself finds instant expression in the invisible world in forms that all creatures, even angels and archangels, can understand.

* Related reading: *Angels and other Mysteries of the Tree of Life,* Izvor No. 236, Chap. 16.

27 January

However great your other achievements, nothing you do will ever have the same importance as your spiritual work, even if at first nobody notices it. For if you respect the rules, the results of your spiritual work will be millions of times more worthwhile than if you worked on a purely practical, utilitarian level. Why? Because you will be working with different values that bestow different rewards.

Imagine someone who is panning for gold – they may find a little bit of gold, maybe even a lot of it. Now imagine an alchemist who works day and night for years on end to find the philosopher's stone,* seemingly in vain. In fact, if he works according to the rules, he will eventually find it, and then he will be able to transform mountains of base metal into gold. By comparison, the amount of gold found by the prospector will be negligible. If I have used the example of alchemy it is not that I want to encourage you to go looking for the philosopher's stone, but because this comparison can give you a good idea of the difference between spiritual work and ordinary work.*

* Related reading: *The Philosopher's Stone in the Gospels and in Alchemy,* Izvor No. 241, Chap. 10.

28 January

Communion* is an abiding, ever-present relationship between the whole of our being and the vital forces of nature: stones, plants, mountains, springs, the sun, the stars, and above all, all living beings. Christians are content to receive communion in church from time to time with bread and wine. But this is not enough. Those who truly know how to communicate are able through their love and wisdom to establish contact with every creature in the universe.

Only when we truly understand this question of communion shall we be able to speak of eating the flesh of Christ and drinking his blood. When this day comes, the true, eternal life that has no beginning and no end will flood into us. Our cells and every dimension of our being will be filled with noble, pure, abundant life.

* Related reading: *The Yoga of Nutrition,* Izvor No. 204, Chap. 8.

29 January

When a disciple loses himself in the contemplation of his Master,* he begins to sense that his Master's face and physical form speak to him of the divine world, that they incite him to link himself to those sublime regions and awaken memories of a distant past in which all was beauty and purity. Through his physical appearance, an Initiate emanates, expresses and reveals the world of the spirit. And it is towards this world that a disciple must work, because it is beautiful, because it is rich, because it is potent and alive.

* Related reading: *What is a Spiritual Master?*, Izvor No. 207, Chap. 8.

30 January

If you want heaven to notice your existence and begin to sustain and help you, you must become rich. 'How can I become rich?' you ask. By working to acquire gold. In the symbolism of initiatic science, gold* represents understanding and wisdom, and you can use this gold to buy qualities and virtues whose presence reveals itself in a radiance of light and colour. Heavenly beings see this radiance from afar and are attracted to it, and this means that if you want entities of the angelic world to accompany you and to help and care for you, you have to be rich. Once you have succeeded in winning their friendship and protection, they will see to it that you have everything you need.

* Related reading: *Light is a Living Spirit,* Izvor No. 212, Chap. 3.

31 January

We are approaching the end of the age of Pisces and entering the Age of Aquarius* in which great changes will occur. This does not mean that the whole of humankind is going to be transformed overnight. What will change for everyone will be their possibilities.

Aquarius is bringing all kinds of new currents into the world, but only those who make an effort to be in harmony with these currents will be transformed. Heaven sends us these waves but it will not force wisdom on us. We are entering the Age of Aquarius, but those who make no effort to benefit from its influence will receive nothing. It is all very well for the name 'Aquarius' to be on everybody's lips, but if you sincerely want to enter the Aquarian age you must prepare yourself to accept the new ideas it brings with it: the ideas of brotherhood and universality.

* Related reading: *A New Dawn: Society and Politics in the Light of Initiatic Science (Part I)*, Complete Works Vol. 25, Chap. 1.

1 February

*H*omeopathic doses do not act on the physical body that much because the particles of which it is made are too compact – massive doses must be given to affect them. However, these doses do act on the etheric, astral and mental bodies whose particles are extremely delicate and subtle.

You will say, 'But how can they then affect the physical body?' Through the intermediary of the other bodies. A look, a word or simply a thought, for example, are homeopathic doses that affect a person's astral and mental bodies, where they set off reactions that eventually reach the physical body. Through the intermediary of the mental, astral and etheric bodies, a look of hatred or a cruel word can actually make a person ill. You have caused such a feeling of distress or horror that it is reflected upon the physical body. Conversely, when someone is dejected, say a few words to them or place your hand on them, and they soon recover! Here too, you have given a homeopathic dose that was received by their subtle bodies and then reflected on their physical body.*

* Related reading: *Man's Psychic Life: Elements and Structures,* Izvor No. 222, Chap. 7.

2 February

*M*en and women's physical appearance does not always correspond to their psyche. There are women who are men on the inside and men who are inwardly women. It also happens that some women are attracted to other women and some men are attracted to other men. This tendency, which is increasingly widespread these days, stems solely from the need each being has to find in another what is lacking in themselves so as to feel complete. Because of this need, they are drawn to what they believe is their complementary pole. The feelings we experience towards a person always matter more than their outer shape.*

* Related reading: *Cosmic Balance, The Secret of Polarity,* Izvor No. 237, Chap. 15.

3 February

*H*uman beings live within the cosmic organism, they are part of it, they are cells in this gigantic body that is the body of the universe, which the Cabbalah refers to as Adam Kadmon, and regardless of what they want or do, they cannot detach themselves from it. They receive life and all the elements they need to subsist from it: food, water, air and light. Of course, if their consciousness does not participate in this reality, they cut themselves off from this organism to a degree and deprive themselves of this life, this support. That is why we must think to attune ourselves everyday with the universe, with the inhabitants of its different regions. Even if we do not know them, even if we do not know where they are, we can make contact with them by means of thought.*

* Related reading: *The Path of Silence*, Izvor No. 229, Chap. 7.

4 February

It requires considerable effort to awaken the powers in you that have lain dormant from centuries of inertia and stagnation. Inertia will not get you anywhere; you will not open any inner doors, activate any forces, nor stir any layers of your psyche into motion. It takes willpower to overcome this inertia. So concentrate, meditate, pray and do exercises.*

Our teaching offers you the best methods with which to overcome the inertia of a mind and heart gripped by darkness and cold. Always seek to add something more to your existence, something brighter and warmer. You should even work by means of thought to impart subtle vibrations to inanimate objects, which will stimulate all those who pass by them beneficially.

* Related reading: *Bringing Symbols to Life – The Gymnastic Exercises,* Stani Coll. No 1.

5 February

*T*he Sphinx of the Egyptians is a representation of the zodiac in relation to the four elements; it has a human head (Aquarius, air sign), the body of an ox (Taurus, earth sign), lion's paws (Leo, fire sign) and the wings of an eagle (Scorpio, water sign). These same figures are found in the Apocalypse of St. John, when he speaks of the four living creatures who stand before the throne of God and who, day and night, without ceasing sing, *'Holy, holy, holy, the Lord God the Almighty, who was and is and is to come!'*

The first of these creatures is like a lion, the second like an ox, the third like a man, and the fourth like an eagle. You will say that in the zodiac there is no eagle but rather a scorpion. In reality, in the primordial zodiac, the Eagle held the place of Scorpio, but this is quite a story that must be understood from a symbolic point of view. As a result of misdirected sexual forces, the Eagle fell and was turned into Scorpio. The Eagle represents a being who could soar very high in the sky, but who fell because he ate of the fruit of the Tree of the Knowledge of Good and Evil.*

* Related reading: *The Zodiac, Key to Man and to the Universe,* Izvor No. 220, Chap. 7.

6 February

Instead of presenting, explaining and exalting moral values, the intellect has separated itself from them and even works against them. In reality, the moral realm* represents the roots of the intellect, which are there to nourish it, fortify it and make it grow. When the intellect is separated from its roots, it crumbles because it cannot feed itself. That is why the intellect is failing in its mission: because it has become detached from the moral realm, from the heart, which represents the roots of life, whereas the intellect represents the branches, leaves, flowers and fruits. This is a magnificent blossoming, of course, it is a splendour, but without its roots, the intellect becomes like a withered branch.

* Related reading: *Cosmic Moral Laws,* Complete Works, Vol. 12.

7 February

Jesus said, *'When you pray, go into your room, shut the door, and pray to your Father who is in the secret place.'* This secret room that Jesus speaks of is a symbol with great depth. Suppose that you are on the street and you would like to talk to a friend who is in another city – you cannot. In order to talk to them, you must go into a phone booth; there, you will find a device, dial a number and your call will go through. If you do not go in, you can talk and you can shout, but your friend will not hear you. Like phone booths, this secret room that Jesus speaks of is well equipped with devices that allow you to communicate with heaven.

Once you have entered the phone booth, you close the door so that you can listen and speak in silence. In the same way, there is also a very silent place within you, and you must shut the door after entering. Shutting the door means not letting thoughts and desires unrelated to the prayer enter into you. At that point, you can address your request to heaven and you will receive an answer.*

* Related reading: *The Powers of Thought,* Izvor No. 224, Chap. 12.

8 February

The fundamental concern of all religions is to help human beings regain the state of peace, joy and light that they enjoyed in the beginning in the bosom of the Lord. They are far less interested in the origin of creation itself, that is to say, the departure from the centre. Moses, for example, wrote only one page to explain how God created the world. Of course, philosophers, theologians and great Initiates have looked into this question, but on the whole, they do not consider it that worthwhile to instruct human beings on this kind of subject. They are collectively much more concerned about getting humans to return to their state of origin by giving them the methods to do so. Human beings strayed from the Source, we know this, and it is not productive to dwell on it; the important thing for them now is to turn back towards it.*

* Related reading: *'Know Thyself' – Jnana Yoga (Part I)*, Complete Works, Vol. 17, Chap.9.

9 February

You cannot yet measure how great a sacrifice a Master makes in agreeing to live among human beings. Human beings, for their part, do not make a sacrifice; they benefit by having a Master, for in this way, they rid themselves of their impurities and imperfections, and the Master gives them pure water and light. For a Master, a saint or an Initiate, accepting to take care of human beings is the greatest sacrifice because he constantly loses through it. Let us rather say that he constantly gives and distributes, but that, fortunately, he is linked to heaven from which he receives divine life. An Initiate gives below and receives from on high. As for the disciples, they endlessly gain: they improve, they are purified, and become more intelligent, more attentive – they acquire a great many qualities thanks to their Master.

Human beings have a tendency to want to obtain everything without being prepared, and this tendency is the cause of many anomalies and catastrophes in the world. Spiritual people are no exception to the rule. They want to begin with what should come only at the end: the acquisition of occult powers. They have not purified themselves, but they are eager to know the greatest secrets in order to use them for their own gain. They will be crushed by these great secrets, which they will not be able to bear, yet they do not see the danger. It is boring to educate, purify and control oneself, so they want the means to obtain everything they crave right away… and there you have candidates for the black lodge! Why do people want everything before they are prepared? Preparation takes a very long time, it can last a whole lifetime, if not several lifetimes, but once someone is truly ready, they can have it all in a few minutes, and what they obtain in this way will make of them a source of blessings.*

* Related reading: *On the Art of Teaching (Part III)*, Complete Works, Vol. 29, Chap.7.

11 February

Someone comes to you and says, 'Oh, what a beautiful violin you have there, please give it to me!' If you are wise, you will say, 'No, I will not give you my violin, it is mine, but come every day and I will play it for you.' But are you wise? So many young girls and young boys give away their violin – their heart – and then, having no heart left, they cry, 'What have you done with my heart?' They should not have given their heart away. Yes, a young girl gives her heart to a boy, but since he is clumsy, he drops it, leaving her to cry over a broken heart. If she had been smart, she would have understood that as the boy already had a heart, he did not need a second one. In Bulgaria, we say that you cannot carry two watermelons under one arm. So hold on to your heart. Give others your good sentiments, but keep your heart, give it only to the Lord for he will not drop it.

* Related reading: *Man's Psychic Life: Elements and Structures,* Izvor No. 222, Chap. 4.

12 February

*T*o become good educators, parents must think about all the qualities and virtues that are buried in the soul and spirit of their child. Instead of merely lecturing or spanking their child for misbehaviour, they must focus on the divine spark that dwells in him, and give it every opportunity to manifest itself, so that the child will later do wonders. And even when the child is already asleep, they can sit by his bed, stroke him gently without waking him, and speak to him about all the good qualities they would like him to manifest later in life. In this way, they place precious elements in his subconscious, which, when they appear years later, will protect him from many mistakes and dangers.*

* Related reading: *Youth: Creators of the Future,* Izvor No. 233.

13 February

When you are able to move an object harmoniously, you activate beneficial forces within yourself that will eventually act favourably upon others as well. So if you are interested in magic, do not go looking for it in rituals or spellbooks – it is right there within reach, in your gestures. The day you learn to master your gestures, you will become a true white magus.

True magic is not about acting upon others, but acting first upon oneself and it is based on the slightest gestures of everyday life. If you do not start by mastering your gestures, you will never know white magic. On the other hand, you can be certain that you will be constantly at risk of conducting black magic. So be careful: you will always be the first to reap the beneficial or evil effects of your gestures, even if you make them unconsciously.*

* Related reading: *The Path of Silence,* Izvor No. 229, Chap. 4.

14 February

Love without expecting to be loved – you will be free and you will be able to do a great deal with this freedom. Unfortunately, human beings do not value freedom, they do not seek it; on the contrary, they want to chain themselves down. It is as if they do not know what to do with freedom, it weighs on them or bores them. Whereas constraints and even blows at least keep them occupied: yes, suffering and crying…

Only the Initiates have resolved the problem. They say, 'But who is preventing me from continuing to love, to love all creatures day and night, to love like the sun?' They are not interested in knowing on whom this love may come to rest – on anyone and everyone. What does interest them is for this divine energy to flow through them so that they may feel expansive, filled with wonder and inspired: that is the only thing that matters.*

* Related reading: *Sexual Force or the Winged Dragon*, Izvor No. 205, Chap. 6.

15 February

Whatever difficulties you face, do not show your sadness and discouragement, do not look gloomy – on the contrary, try to make the light shine within you. Yes, the worse things get, the more you must shine the light. For do you know what will happen as a result? Everyone will come from all sides asking, 'Do you need anything? What can I get you?' You will even have a surfeit of services offered to you, simply because of your light!

You believe that your misfortunes can touch people's hearts, so you tell them about your woes, and you exaggerate, adding aches and pains in the hope that they will finally decide to help you out. However, they have only one desire: to get rid of you as quickly as possible! Yes, unfortunately that is the way it is. People rarely come to help you in such cases, because only beauty, light and love attract human beings. So, the worse things get, the more radiant and joyful you must become.*

* Related reading: *The Tree of the Knowledge of Good and Evil,* Izvor No. 210, Chap. 10.

16 February

You must learn to live in the world, have a relationship with it, while putting what is most important first: the soul and the spirit. An individual's intelligence, love and willpower are revealed by the way in which they reconcile their inner life and their life in the world, and nothing is more difficult than this. For some people, the temptation is to immerse themselves in the material life, forgetting about the life of the spirit, while others are involved only with the life of the spirit, forgetting about the material life.

There is, however, a third solution and everyone must find it for themselves, because each case is different. Someone who feels compelled to start a family cannot resolve the question in the same way as someone who prefers to stay single. Someone who needs a lot of physical activity cannot lead the same life as someone who has a meditative, contemplative temperament. You will say, 'So we can't take anyone as a role model?' Yes, you can, but only in a broader sense, not in terms of the details. Everyone has their own path to follow, their own mission, and even if you take your Master as a role model, you must still evolve according to your own nature.*

* Related reading: 'Know Thyself' – Jnana Yoga (Part I), Complete Works, Vol. 17, Chap.6

17 February

Nature does not tolerate lazy people. Each of us must be engaged and mobilized in work; a particle that wanders about idly is not tolerated, it must be part of a whole, of a system. Those who wander around aimlessly, without direction, end up falling prey to dark forces, and soon find themselves living in hell. So you always have to fight against inertia and, one way or another, decide to set to work.

The meaning of life is found in work. Some say that it is love, others power, study or pleasure. That may be so, of course, but for a true Initiate it is work, work directed towards a divine goal. Beware of anything that is not directed towards a divine purpose, for wherever the Lord does not enter, the devil will.*

* Related reading: *The Powers of Thought,* Izvor No. 224, Chap. 1.

18 February

As soon as God created the first man and the first woman, He gave them a name, and He instructed them to name the animals and plants themselves. A name represents, summarizes and contains the entity that bears it. When a being succeeds in elevating themselves to a higher degree of consciousness, they are given a new name. This is because they are a regenerated being. By means of its vibrations, the new name conferred upon the regenerated person expresses exactly the quintessence of their spiritual being. Every man and every woman has a name given to them by their parents at birth, but most of the time, this name does not mean much. Whereas the name they are given by the celestial entities is the one that corresponds exactly to them, that expresses exactly what they are in the depths of their being.*

* Related reading: *The Book of Revelation: a Commentary,* Izvor No. 230, Chap. 5.

19 February

*R*id yourself of the need you still have to be valued, appreciated and coddled for it is this need that prevents you from developing properly. You are offended by the smallest things simply because you have not been treated with the consideration you think you deserve. Why all the fuss? You are all sons and daughters of God, isn't that enough for you? No, you fret and torment yourselves because human beings – who are often idiots – do not sing your praises!

You can tell right away from people's faces what they are after; and for many it is clear that they want to be bowed down to and recognized as the centre of the universe. As long as they nurture this desire instead of trying to fight it, they will not be able to move forward. Let them forget about themselves a little and they will see how free they will feel.*

* Related reading: *On the Art of Teaching (Part III)*, Complete Works, Vol. 29, Chap.4.

20 February

In the book of *Zohar*, it is said that Libra is at the origin of creation to show that all the forces of nature are perfectly balanced. In reality, there is no such thing as absolute equilibrium; there is a constant fluctuation, for if the two pans of the scales remained perfectly steady, no manifestation would be possible. It is due to this slight imbalance that the forces flow, that everything is in motion. However, neither pan must sink too low for then it all tips over leading to total destruction.

An example of this law is seen in the field of psychology. Compared to ordinary men, geniuses can be considered unbalanced, which is why it is said that there is a fine line between a lunatic and a genius. A genius knows how to work with opposing forces and remain in a creative imbalance, whereas a lunatic goes a bit too far.*

* Related reading: *The Splendour of Tiphareth – The Yoga of the Sun,* Complete Works, Vol. 10, Chap.11.

21 February

*E*ach of us has the ability to wish fervently, to ask insistently, and that is what prayer is. You do not have to be very intelligent or educated to call out to heaven; you simply need to have an intense feeling. Which is why, if someone is hesitant to undertake a spiritual life on the pretext that they do not have the necessary abilities and qualities, you can say, 'When you are unhappy or suffering, don't you concentrate on getting rid of your misery? Don't you ask for help? Well that is all it takes.'

Everyone has the ability to concentrate and to cry out for help, and these are the abilities that matter most for our evolution, for our spiritual progress. Indeed, it may well be that the poor, the destitute, the unfortunate and the dying have more power of prayer than others who are numbed by success and material well-being.

In the Lord's Prayer, Jesus says, *'Thy kingdom come, Thy will be done on earth as it is in heaven...'* With these words, Jesus tells human beings that it is their task to transform, beautify and purify the earth so that one day it becomes like heaven. They must not flee from the world and its difficulties because it suits them to save their 'little soul', but rather undertake the glorious work of bringing about heaven on earth. You will say, 'But how? It can't be done!' Yes, it can.

It is true that a spiritual person must seek heaven, but once they have reached it, they must also remember to bring the light of heaven, the love of heaven, the power of heaven and the purity of heaven, down into their brain, their lungs, their stomach – into their whole body. This is how, after years of effort, they will be able to achieve the union of spirit and matter within themselves.

23 February

*T*he act of lovemaking is in itself neither good nor bad, it is simply what you make it. If you have not done any work to purify, ennoble and enlighten yourself, you will pass on diseases, vices and harmful influences to your partner through this act. True love should improve everything in the being you love – it should uplift, strengthen and illuminate them. It is only when you see that the person is blossoming thanks to your love that you can be happy and thank heaven for having been able to help and protect them.*

* Related reading: *The Mysteries of Yesod,* Complete Works, Vol. 7, Chap.2.

24 February

*H*eaven observes how you regard the truths that a Master brings you. A Master is like an envoy, an ambassador who represents a great country – heaven – and by respecting him, you show that you also respect the country that sent him. Heaven inspires your Master to tell you what is needed for your progress, and if you do not take his words seriously, how do you expect to convince heaven of your respect and love? You will not be able to, and then, upon seeing your carelessness, heaven will withdraw its help.

In order to attract heaven's benevolence, you must start from the beginning: you must take its envoys seriously. You do not realize how many spirits have undertaken to help you through your Master. Yes, thousands of entities have come to help you along your path of evolution, and if you fail to give all this proper consideration, too bad for you, you will gain nothing.*

* Related reading: *Life and Work in an Initiatic School – Training for the Divine,* Complete Works, Vol. 30, Chap.5.

25 February

*I*magine that you leave home in the morning to go to work and along the way, you meet a hundred people, each of whom greets you with a look full of light and love – in what state would you be then?

Unfortunately, the reality is quite the opposite; so many of the people we meet in the street give us such expressionless or hostile looks that we are demagnetized. One wonders how these people behave with their families, and moreover, how their families ever put up with them! Why are we so stingy with a smile, a kind look or anything that can bring harmony? What do you have to lose by giving something of yourself every now and then? You do not know what riches you possess let alone how to distribute them.*

* Related reading: *The Path of Silence,* Izvor No. 229, Chap. 7.

26 February

Studying alchemy, magic, astrology and the Cabbalah can help you to progress more quickly along the path of evolution, and to fathom the meaning of the greatest mysteries. However, to understand these sciences properly, you must first begin by studying them in relation to man and the activities of daily life. For we can discover alchemy in nutrition, astrology in our breathing, magic in our words and gestures, and the Cabbalah in our thoughts.

Therefore, learn how to eat, breathe, act, speak and think, and you will acquire the basics of these four fundamental sciences. You should not try to approach esoteric science by detaching it from life.*

* Related reading: *The Second Birth,* Complete Works, Vol. 1, Chap. 5.

27 February

We would not be able to do anything were it not for the legacy left to us by the great Initiates; without them, our steps are faltering. What could present-day researchers do without the tremendous legacy passed down to them by the physicists, chemists and astronomers of the past? Imagine if a chemist still had to try to discover the electrolysis of water before setting to work on their research... We are fortunate to have a patrimony on the physical plane, which we recognize; but we forget the patrimony we have received in the spiritual realm. This is why we must link ourselves to the Initiates and the great Masters.

What can we achieve by ourselves, relying solely on our own very limited experience and our inadequate personal efforts? Nothing, because we are weak and blind. We must rely on the beings who are above us, the great Masters of truth, so that they may impart to us their experience, the extent of which is inconceivable, and through them be united with the truth, with Christ and with the Lord.*

* Related reading: *Alchemy, Astrology, Magic, Kabbalah – Aspects of Esoteric Science,* Complete Works, Vol. 4, Chap. 5.

28 February

If the true order of things were respected on earth, all those who are inwardly poor would be poor on the outside too, just as those who are inwardly rich would be rich on the outside. Like the Lord. The Lord, who possesses all the qualities and virtues, also possesses all the riches of the universe.

It is only here, among human beings, that this order no longer exists, but since the law is absolute (that which is below must be like that which is above, that which is on the outside must be like that which is on the inside), one day, everyone will find their place. Those who possess a wealth of intelligence, goodness and nobleness will also possess all the corresponding outer riches, and those who do not possess these qualities will be destitute. Obviously, it will not be up to human beings to re-establish this order, because they do not know who is deserving and who is not. It will be the work of Cosmic Intelligence, for the law of correspondences is an immutable law in the universe.

1 March

Those who have made a profound study of the relationship between human beings and the forces of nature have discovered that there is an absolute correspondence between them. As every vibration tends to detect and fuse with other matching vibrations, every creature, by reason of its particular vibrations, its particular wavelength, is in communication with other entities and currents in the cosmos whose wavelengths and vibrations are identical. So, by virtue of their thoughts, feelings and actions, a person creates an affinity with entities and regions of the cosmos with the same wavelength, and sooner or later, the force of attraction inevitably brings them together.

The light of Initiatic Science gives us the keys we need to create the destiny and the future we desire. Depending on the quality of our thoughts, feelings and desires, we are drawn towards beautiful, luminous, noble beings or, on the contrary, we topple into hell.*

* Related reading: *Cosmic Moral Laws,* Complete Works, Vol. 12, Chap. 16.

2 March

From the beginning of time, geometricians have struggled in vain to solve the problem of squaring the circle; that is to say, how to draw a square with exactly the same area as a given circle. Perhaps they will solve the problem one day, but they should know that Initiates did so long ago. Thanks to their skill in observing nature, particularly trees, Initiates saw how the bare branches are periodically clothed in leaves, flowers and fruit.

Periodically the spirit appears and accomplishes a certain task; this is the circle, the symbol of the limitless, infinite universe. And it is within this circle that the square (matter) can flower and bear fruit each time the spirit returns. When a tree that has been vivified by the spirit bears fruit, it has solved the squaring the circle. Sooner or later, there comes a time when the circle and the square coincide.*

* Related reading: *The Symbolic Language of Geometrical Figures,* Izvor No. 218, Chap. 2 and 7.

3 March

*F*or disciples of Initiatic Science, old age is the best period in life, for their years of searching and inner experience have brought them lucidity, peace, serenity and kindness. If popular opinion is in direct contradiction to this, it is because old age is, in fact, an unhappy time for many people as a result of the way they have lived. They have squandered all their energies in mundane, futile, stupid activities and, when they have almost nothing left and then find themselves debilitated, ill and barren, what can they hope for in their old age?

Of course, even if you lead a sensible life, old age will eventually catch up with you and perhaps illness as well. But those who have done some serious inner work will face these periods with greater strength and serenity and continue to grow spiritually richer.*

* Related reading: *The Seeds of Happiness,* Izvor No. 231, Chap. 8.

4 March

Think of the mountains, of their forests, lakes and peaks, but also of their deep caverns and the entities who dwell in them, so that you can always be on friendly terms with them. Mountains are not just piles of earth and rock; they are treasure houses of immense wealth in which gold, silver, crystals and precious stones are produced and watched over by powerful entities. I am not saying this with the idea that you should take it literally and go off to dig holes in the mountains in the hope of finding these treasures. It is the symbolic, living aspect of the mountains that you must focus on; whose heights you must climb and whose depths you must probe within yourselves to find spiritual treasures there.*

* Related reading: *The Mysteries of Fire and Water,* Izvor No. 232, Chap. 7.

5 March

When someone indulges in excesses and leads a disorderly life, we say that they are burning the candle at both ends. Although most people know and use this expression, they do not pay much attention to the way they make use of their energies. On the contrary, because of the disorder of their lives, they burn their candle at both ends. They imagine that their supply of energy is endless and will automatically be replenished. Certain elements can indeed be replaced, because Cosmic Intelligence has designed the human organism in such a way that it can repair and replace some of what it uses as it goes along. But when someone behaves unreasonably, the losses are irreparable. Those who live in a state of disorder and passion waste their most precious energies, and in doing so, not only do they deprive their psychic and spiritual bodies of nourishment, but they also weaken their physical bodies.*

* Related reading: *The Mysteries of Fire and Water,* Izvor No. 232, Chap. 2.

6 March

Someone says, 'Ah, if only I had a crust of bread I'd be happy. I would ask for nothing more!' So you give them some bread, but then they say, 'How marvellous it would be if I had a drop of wine; life would be complete!' So you give them a bottle of wine. 'Now, if only I had a cigarette that would be great!' You give them a cigarette. 'If only I had a pretty girl!' It never ends!

You need to eat, drink and sleep, to have a roof over your head and clothes to wear; you need to work, go out and about, read, listen to music, meet other people, reflect, admire things, and so on. Cosmic Intelligence has organized things in this way because it wants human beings to develop in every domain and on every plane. As soon as you feel a new need, a new problem arises – and then another and another and another. Our whole life is a series of exercises we have to do in order to find the solutions to all these problems.

7 March

The most effective way to draw an entity to oneself is to say their name. This is why the Kabbalah gives the names of the seventy-two Planetary Spirits, for each of them has a specific function and we can call on their help in the various circumstances of life.

To pronounce the name of an entity is not insignificant, for the vibrations of a name put you directly in touch with the entity concerned. It is possible in this way to make contact with all the spirits of the universe and, through this contact, draw their qualities into oneself. So, be very careful about what name you pronounce, for if it is that of a fiend, you will attract all sorts of difficulties and misfortunes to yourself. Yes, a name is extremely important. There are instances when you can be saved from danger by pronouncing the name of a being whose only desire is to help humans.*

* Related reading: *On the Art of Teaching (Part III)*, Complete Works, Vol. 29, Chap. 6.

8 March

Suffering gives humans an opportunity to enter into their own depths and reflect, meditate and draw to themselves higher beings who can guide and help them. If you suffer knowing that it is through your suffering that heaven wants to transform you, you will become an exceptional being. There is no greater science than the knowledge of how to suffer. The suffering of flowers is their scent; because of all the difficulties they have to overcome in order to withstand bad weather and endure despite all the dangers that threaten them, flowers give off an exquisite scent and we love them for it.

Not all suffering distils such exquisite scents, for most human beings do not know how to suffer; they cry out at the slightest pang. Only those who have learned to accept suffering exhale this scent. When an Initiate suffers because they have taken upon themself the burdens and sins of other men, as Jesus did, this suffering accepted out of love produces the most exquisite perfume. The angels gather round them to delight in it, just as we delight in the scent of a blossoming tree in a garden.*

* Related reading: *Love Greater Than Faith,* Izvor No. 239, Chap. 7.

9 March

If things happened according to our wishes, the results would often be disastrous. We are not clear-sighted enough to see the long-term consequences of what we wish for. If the things we believe to be for our good all came to pass, we would end by living a life of idleness and pleasure.

It is just as well that Cosmic Intelligence does not grant human beings the kind of happiness they want, for they would lose everything, even the taste for life. For true happiness lies in the efforts we make. So stop looking for things that are sweet and sugary, for they will only make you sick. The day you develop a taste for bitterness, for quinine, you will be on the road to salvation. Do not cry for the things you like and cannot have, for they are often the very things that would make you ill. It is heaven that deprives you of them, so that you may live a little longer.*

* Related reading: *The Path of Silence,* Izvor No. 229.

10 March

It is not by being selfish and careless that you will best defend your interests. On the contrary, it is in your interest to think of others, for in doing so you improve the conditions of your own life. Let us take an example: you are walking down a path when you come across a lot of broken glass, and you leave it there, thinking, 'After all, it's not my fault if it's there. Somebody else can sweep it up!' Then, later that night, fate sends you home by the same path. You have forgotten about the glass, and you step on it in the dark and hurt yourself. Then, of course, you exclaim, 'What idiot left broken glass lying around? What a criminal thing to do!' Yes, but it is too late to ask yourself that; you should have swept it up the first time you went by.*

* Related reading: *The Seeds of Happiness,* Izvor No. 231, Chap. 15.

11 March

We must learn to be constantly connected to the Source, to slake our thirst with the water of love that fills the universe and in which we are immersed. We are often like a man standing up to his neck in water who cries out, 'I'm thirsty! Give me water!' He only has to open his mouth and drink, but he keeps it shut tight and dies of thirst.* Although this love surrounds us and washes over us, everyone continues to look for it, continues to sigh and moan for it.

'In him we live and move and have our being', says St Paul. Without realizing it, we are immersed in love just as fish are immersed in the waters of the ocean. We need only to create a few small openings in ourselves to be immediately flooded with this extraordinary force of love.

* Related reading: *New Light on the Gospels,* Izvor No. 217, Chap. 10.

12 March

It is normal for human beings always to want to possess more and to compete with others. At what point does it become abnormal? Our own bodies give us the answer so clearly that no one can deny it. What does your stomach do when you give it food? It takes only what it needs, and even the little it keeps is not exclusively for its own benefit; it works on it before distributing it to the rest of the body. So, the stomach retains what it needs for only a short time, and if it lets you know that it wants more after a few hours, it does not ask for more than it really needs.

Our health depends on the wise behaviour of our stomach. But suppose your stomach were to say, 'From now on, I'm going to keep everything for myself. Why should I bother about all those other idiots? Besides, who knows what the future holds; I've got my offspring to think of.' Well, if it hoards all the food for itself, you will soon be very ill. If human beings would only reflect a little, they would see that they were behaving like selfish stomachs, thereby endangering the health of the immense body of humanity.*

* Related reading: *A New Dawn: Society and Politics in the Light of Initiatic Science (Part I),* Complete Works, Vol. 25, Chap. 4.

13 March

*E*ven if you manage to improve your material circumstances, after a brief moment of satisfaction, you will fall back into the same state of dissatisfaction, bitterness and revolt, until you finally decide to do some real inner work.

Psychic shortcomings cannot be assuaged on the physical plane. We can go on forever stockpiling medicines, wealth and power, but if our psychic and spiritual life is in poor condition, we will never know true satisfaction. It is in our soul and thoughts, in our perception of the world, in our point of view and the way we reason that we must change something. Otherwise, however much you accumulate in the way of possessions, you will end up only being jaded and disgusted.*

* Related reading: *Love Greater Than Faith,* Izvor No. 239, Chap. 9.

14 March

*Y*our Master is meditating. The best thing you can do in this case is to meditate too. 'Yes, but the meditation was too long today!' This is because your Master is better able than you to sense when conditions are favourable and to make use of them. You must try to do the same. If your Master does something you do not understand, do not argue or criticize or be up in arms about it; do as he does. One day you will understand, but in the meantime, imitate him and in this way, you will develop your intelligence.

Why do you suppose someone wrote a book called 'The Imitation of Christ'? Precisely because it is by imitating those who are far more advanced than ourselves that we can best grow and develop. And if we persevere, we too shall be capable of doing exactly what these great beings did.

15 March

In our Teaching, there is a reason for everything, however small and apparently insignificant. Take the example of the short pauses between each song or the silence we observe at meals. You do not yet sufficiently appreciate all these occasions that are given to you to reach a state of peace and unite yourselves to the world of harmony. Yet you can sense that the hectic pace of your daily lives is playing havoc with your nervous system. Human beings were not made to live in a perpetual state of tension that burns up all their energies. It is not normal always to have to hustle and hurry. In the long run the nervous system breaks down.

When we are together, working to create an atmosphere of love and harmony, each one of us is in contact with their higher Self, and this higher Self projects rays into our cells that have a beneficial effect on our health. Many ailments can be cured in this way. This is why you must take advantage of all these moments of silence in order to recover your inner peace and balance.*

* Related reading: *A Philosophy of Universality,* Izvor No. 206.

16 March

The four states of matter – solid, liquid, gaseous and igneous – are all present in our everyday activities. The solid state is represented by our actions; the liquid state by our feelings; the gaseous state by our thoughts; and the igneous, etheric state by the activity of our soul and spirit.

Each of these four states, which are related to the four elements, corresponds symbolically to a specific trial in our life. The solid state corresponds to earthquakes, the liquid state to torrential rain and floods, the gaseous state to hurricanes and storms, and the igneous state to fires and lightning. If you think about this, you will find that accidents of this nature really do occur in your psychic life. If you want to overcome such trials, you must work to strengthen your will, purify your heart, illuminate your intellect, and sanctify your soul and spirit.*

* Related reading: *Man's Psychic Life: Elements and Structures,* Izvor No. 222, Chap. 4.

17 March

*T*he purity and transparency of a person's aura depend on the way they live. If they are materialistic and spiritually lazy, their aura will be like a cloud and give off foul odours that others perceive; even if they do not see anything (for it is very difficult for anyone who is not clairvoyant to see a person's aura), they sense a dark, heavy atmosphere like that of a swamp.

Whereas an Initiate, a Master, who has worked for hundreds and thousands of years to cultivate all the virtues (love, wisdom, purity and disinterestedness), has an immense aura in which all creatures can immerse themselves and feel nourished, pacified, strengthened and oriented towards God.

18 March

The day you succeed in reproducing within yourself the image of God, the spirits of nature and the four elements will be your servants. If you ask them for something, they will be happy to grant it, because they can see this image in you and it is the only one that commands their respect. If they cannot see that image, not only will they oppose you, but they may even destroy you. This is how many black magicians who tried to command the spirits of nature became their victims – the spirits sought revenge and tore them apart, for they hate to obey people who have no love, purity or light, and who try to impose their will on them by means of magic spells. The only power they respect is the light projected by an Initiate who has succeeded in reproducing within themself the authentic image of God.*

* Related reading: *The Book of Divine Magic,* Izvor No. 226.

19 March

We often hear people say, 'I lost my head!' Yes, they lose all control, they do not know what they are doing or saying – they lose their heads. Of course, the head is just a symbol; they could equally well speak of the heart, for the heart is also a vital centre in man.

But whether they speak of the heart or the head, what people really lose in these instances is their link with the divine world, which coordinates all their activities and all the different elements within them. As a result, the disorder spreads; everything flies apart. When the cells of your body hear that the head, the boss, is no longer in charge, they all take the opportunity to break out in revolt against the rule of law, and instead of being your obedient servants, they become dangerous enemies who are ready to kill you. You end up in bed and they chuckle in delight, 'Aha, that will teach you not to sever your ties with heaven!' But as soon as you return to the centre, to the spirit, they start working harmoniously again.*

* Related reading: *Under the Dove, the Reign of Peace,* Izvor No. 208, Chap. 9.

20 March

A tree has roots, a trunk and branches, but it is not really a tree until the spirit has started to work within it so that it can produce leaves, flowers and fruit.* The same is true of human beings. They have a stomach, lungs and a brain, but these are not enough for them to manifest themselves fully as a human being. Like the roots, trunk and branches of a tree, their organs are no more than the material form and support through which the spirit works to bring forth leaves, flowers and fruit. Leaves are for the stomach, flowers for the lungs, and fruit for the head. The descent of the spirit into someone is like the advent of spring, which gives a tree the opportunity to display all its hidden treasures.

* Related reading: *The Symbolic Language of Geometrical Figures,* Izvor No. 218, Chap. 9.

21 March

Electricity is the type of heating that corresponds symbolically to initiates, to those who know how to get all their inner instruments to function by plugging directly into the current from heaven. They turn on the switch and immediately feel the life-giving warmth.

Others – the majority of human beings – warm themselves by burning wood, coal or oil, that is to say, their feelings and emotions, and every day they have to clean out the ashes and cinders and add more fuel to the fire. Yes, most people have to tend their fires continually and with meagre results. Even when their unbridled passions work up a great blaze, they are still cold. Yet, from the very beginning, each human being possesses a well-equipped furnace and all the fuel they need. It is just that most people still lack the match, the spark of the spirit that will make the flame spring forth: contact with the divine world.*

* Related reading: *The Mysteries of Fire and Water,* Izvor No. 232, Chap. 14.

22 March

It is up to you to have a rich, full, happy life, but for this, you must learn to open yourselves and become inwardly more generous. Why are you so stingy? Why do you always wait for others to take the first step, to be the first to say hello or to smile at you? You must not wait. It is up to you to project always more light and love, to perfume the air around you with your fragrance. If you do this, even the pebbles on the ground will start to quiver, and all those who approach you will feel that an unknown vibration is entering their being.

Humans are capable of animating and spiritualizing matter, not only the matter of their own cells, but also that of nature, even of stones. But they cannot do this if they expect everything to come from others. They must learn to tear particles of light and love from their own heart and soul.

23 March

We must all turn towards the sun, this universal principle that is the source of all religions, and steep ourselves in its example. Every day the sun gives light, warmth and life to every creature that exists: this is the religion of the sun. The sun was there even before human beings appeared on earth, and from the beginning it has always told them, 'Get rid of your narrow notions and do as I do. Use your intelligence and your love to enfold the whole world in light, warmth and life.'

The one true religion is the solar religion, which teaches us how to become luminous, warm and life-giving. It teaches us how to work to acquire the wisdom that illuminates and solves problems; the disinterested love that embellishes, encourages and consoles; the subtle, spiritual life that makes us active, dynamic and intrepid in order to bring about the kingdom of God and His justice on earth. No one can stand up against this religion. Those who attempt to combat it destroy themselves by limiting themselves.*

* Related reading: *Toward a Solar Civilization,* Izvor No. 201.

24 March

What is a civilization? It is a product of water. Yes, just look at where humans have made their homes from time immemorial: near water. Where there is water, plants and animals make their appearance, and human beings build their dwellings. But water can be understood on different levels. It can also represent love, and in the absence of love, everything is a desert.

Unfortunately, most people never think that love is necessary in order to build something; they rely exclusively on organization. And this is where they go wrong, for without life, without love, which is the true driving force, nothing will work. As soon as love is there, even with no organization, everything falls into place.*

* Related reading: *The Mysteries of Fire and Water,* Izvor No. 232, Chap. 4.

25 March

When faced with questions of a spiritual order, scientists should say, 'The present state of our knowledge does not allow us to provide the answer. We need to study more and find other methods of investigation.' This would be the only reasonable attitude, but instead of this, they pass judgement and lead humanity astray by taking themselves and their own limited understanding as the universal yardstick.

How is it that when an explorer tells of their travels to the ends of the earth and describes the countries, mountains and animals they have seen, everybody believes them? Yet they refuse to believe those who have visited other, spiritual regions and who come back to tell of their travels! Explorers and anthropologists could very well be lying, but people believe them; however, nobody trusts the explorers of the invisible world. Why is this? Well, there are some surprises in store for conventional science, for one day it will be forced to stand up for the truths taught by Initiatic Science.*

---

* Related reading: *Looking into the Invisible,* Izvor No. 228, Chap. 1.

26 March

What force is it that teaches you how to look at someone you love with great tenderness, how to caress them, be good to them and give them presents? And what force is it that tells you how to look daggers or hit someone you are angry with? Whether it is love or anger, it is the same force. Sometimes it manifests itself gently in the Venusian manner, with poetic expressiveness and delicacy. Sometimes it expresses itself in a Martian manner and can be terrifying. But it is always the same force.

This becomes obvious when love, manifested on too low a level, turns into violence. The person tries to impose their own will, becomes harsh and cruel, and seeks to satisfy their own appetites and desires without consideration for the other. Of course, this kind of love is not very aesthetic, neither is it beneficial, generous or divine. But if your love is of a higher degree, you will be obliged to behave with tenderness and delicacy and to show much more consideration for the present and future happiness of the one you love. This is the only difference.*

* Related reading: *Love and Sexuality (Part II)*, Complete Works, Vol. 15, Chap. 19.

27 March

If prayer is to be truly effective, it must be expressed in the three worlds: physical, astral and mental.* If it remains exclusively in the world of thought, it will not produce results on the physical plane. Thoughts have to be expressed in words in order to affect the physical plane through the vibrations of sound. If you fail to give your prayer words (flesh), it will only have a soul, and that soul must then look for the physical and astral elements it needs in order to materialize.

But if the thought in your mind is accompanied and nourished by a powerful sentiment and launched onto the physical plane by means of speech, it will have the best chance of being realized, for you will have given the spirits the physical elements that they themselves lack. In this way, you show them that you know the laws and you also make their work easier.

* See note and figure on p. 394 and p. 395.

28 March

*A*ll human beings want happiness but they do not know how to go about it. They do not even know that there is work to be done and a discipline to be observed in order to obtain it. Just because they are here on earth, they think that they only need to eat, drink, sleep, go out, potter around and have children to be automatically happy. But animals do much the same things, so what is the difference? To be on earth is no guarantee of happiness. If you want to be happy, there are a certain number of things you must do... and a certain number of things you must not do!

If you want to find happiness, go out and look for the elements that nourish it. These elements belong to the divine world, and once you find them, not only will you love everyone and be loved in return, but you will also understand things better and have the power to act and to achieve your aspirations.*

* Related reading: *The Seeds of Happiness,* Izvor No. 231.

Your only concern must be to live a pure, intense, luminous life, and it is this life that will take care of attracting beneficial beings who will love you and help you. Just live that life and let it do its work. You have no idea of the lengths it can go to to gather kindred entities around you. Live that life and one day you will exclaim, 'I never asked for my soulmate, I never looked for my beloved, and yet they came to me. From the far reaches of the universe they came to me!'

How difficult it is to get human beings to understand this! Their emanations contain none of the good or luminous elements capable of attracting the marvellous being they long for, so they advertise in the newspapers and go in search of their soulmate in an endless round of parties, and even in nightclubs. And what they find – all too easily – does not bear thinking of!

30 March

*T*he subconscious is a region of darkness rather like the depths of the ocean, and it is dangerous to dive into it without the proper equipment, for there are monsters in its depths that will devour you.

'Where can you get the right equipment?' you ask. Well, that is not so easy. The necessary equipment can be found only in the region of the superconscious, which is on a higher level than consciousness and self-consciousness. Before diving into the subconscious you have to rise to the level of the superconscious, for it is only there that you can learn all you need to know about the structure of those obscure regions and the nature of the entities that dwell in them. Also, it is on this elevated plane that you can develop a powerful will and a luminous aura that will enable you to descend into the abyss without endangering yourself. The lower spirits will only give way before you if they see that you are properly instructed and well armed.*

* Related reading: *Man's Psychic Life: Elements and Structures,* Izvor No. 222, Chap. 12.

31 March

*M*any fairy tales tell of a beautiful princess who is held captive by a dragon in a castle full of treasure. Several knights come forward and try to deliver the princess but they are all vanquished by the dragon. Then one day, a valiant knight appears who is younger, purer and more handsome than all the others, to whom a good fairy, who knows all the dragon's weaknesses, has confided a secret that will enable him to vanquish it. So, the knight defeats the dragon and releases the princess from captivity, and then how sweet are their kisses! All the treasure that has been stored up for centuries in the castle now belongs to the handsome knight whose courage, knowledge and love have brought him victory. And the knight and the princess set out to explore the world mounted on the fire-breathing dragon.

This story is actually very profound. It is an allegory of man and his psychic life. The dragon represents sexual energy, the castle is man's body with all the treasures it contains, and the princess is his soul. The knight is man's ego, which has to deliver his soul from prison. Finally, the knight's weapons are the means man has at his disposal – will-power and knowledge – in order to master his sexual energy and make it his servant.*

* Related reading: *Sexual Force or the Winged Dragon,* Izvor No. 205, Chap. 1.

1 April

You must pay attention to your actions, of course, but never lose sight of the fact that our thoughts and feelings are what is most important, for they are the real forces. Actions are but the result, the consequence of movements arising much higher up in the heart, the intellect, the soul or the spirit. The root of everything that happens on the physical plane is not on the physical plane but much further away, much higher up. This is true for the earth, the forms of which are shaped by the action of the sun, air and water, but it is also true for our actions, which depend on our thoughts and feelings.

This is why you should place much more importance on the quality of your thoughts and feelings than on that of your actions, for as long as your thoughts and feelings are inspired by wisdom and love, your actions will also be inspired by wisdom and love.

2 April

Simply because they are creatures, human beings are linked to every created thing in the universe. This means that every human being is bound by invisible, etheric bonds to animals, plants and rocks, as well as to the angels and archangels.* There is no need to ask why this is: it just is. There is not a speck of dust, not a single cell, not an electron in the universe that is not linked by its vibrations to the whole universe. In spite of appearances, separateness does not exist; it is an illusion. No single thing, no single being is a separate entity. Even if we are unaware of it, we are constantly linked to the whole cosmos.

* Related reading: *On the Art of Teaching (Part III)*, Complete Works, Vol. 29, Chap. 2.

3 April

*T*hose who live with intensity are able to vibrate on the same wavelength as light, or even more rapidly,* for though it is true that on the physical plane light vibrates more rapidly than anything else, on the etheric, astral and mental planes, humans can attain speeds that are far greater still. By means of their thoughts, of their spirit they can travel millions of miles per second. The light of the sun takes eight minutes to reach the earth, whereas thought can reach the farthest corner of the universe instantaneously. The movement of the spirit is much faster than that of light, but in the physical world, light is the example we must follow; it is light that teaches us how to intensify the movement of life.

* Related reading: *Light is a Living Spirit,* Izvor No. 212, Chap. 8.

4 April

*E*xcept in very rare cases, human beings need to be influenced and encouraged by others in order to persevere on the right path, for a time always comes when their zeal falters. Of course, some people say that they have no desire to be influenced; that they want to be free to do as they please. This is why they prefer not to join a spiritual brotherhood; they feel it as a constraint. Well, such people are not very intelligent. Intelligent people put themselves in a position where they will be restrained from doing anything foolish, but free to do what is luminous and helpful. When you have the urge to do something foolish, instead of trying to find a situation that will make it easier, you should run to a place where you will be prevented from doing it.

5 April

Nothing can compare to the speed, power, subtlety and purity of light. This is why Initiates, who need to find the best possible image of God, choose light – they can see no better image of God here on earth than the light of the sun.

And in order to link yourself with the Divine, you too should picture a sun shining in space. Send it your thoughts, unite with it and you will see that this sun, God's representative, will raise the vibrations of your very being. All the elements within you will be exalted, and you will be projected into the higher regions of space where you will be safe from torment.*

* Related reading: *Toward a Solar Civilization,* Izvor No. 201.

6 April

Whatever some people may think, bringing up young people to be aware that the world of the soul and spirit is a reality gives different results than when they are deprived of this notion. Life's events will unfold quite differently for them. Of course, they will encounter exactly the same obstacles and difficulties as everyone else, but they will have means, forces and powers at their disposal that those who have lost contact with the divine world do not possess. This means that in circumstances in which others weaken and lose courage or turn away from the path of light, they will continue to advance, improve and bring support and light to those around them.*

* Related reading: *Youth: Creators of the Future*, Izvor No. 233, Chap. 9.

7 April

You have a Master and you follow his teaching, but do not imagine that you will retain anything if you do not strive to make this teaching an intrinsic part of yourself. It is no good repeating, 'Our Master is good, our Master is wise', even if you back up your words with all kinds of quotes. The goodness and wisdom of your Master are his, not yours. If you do not work to make them yours as well, they will be of very little use to you.*

A true disciple is not content to vaunt their Master's virtues or quote his words; they make his teaching their own. They assimilate it so completely that eventually, when they speak about it, they can no longer distinguish between their own thought and that of their Master. This should be a disciple's ideal. If they do not work towards this, even if they follow their Master's teaching for twenty or thirty years, not one scrap of it will be their own. When they come back in a later reincarnation, they will have to study all over again as though they had never had a Master or teaching before.

* Related reading: *Life with the Master Peter Deunov. Autobiographical Reflections 2.*

8 April

In the symbol of Mercury ☿ , the Sun (masculine principle) is represented by a circle, and the Moon (feminine principle) by a segment of a circle, as though it were a rib taken from the Sun. This is why it is said in Genesis that God made Eve from a rib drawn from Adam's side.

Mercury is the combination, the intelligent fusing together of the masculine and feminine principles, and the glyph chosen by the ancient Initiates to express this is the symbol of the Sun joined to that of the Moon by the +, the symbol of Earth. The glyph of Mercury is sufficient proof of the profound science of the Initiates. One of its numerous variants, the caduceus of Hermes, represented by two serpents entwined round a central rod, has remained to this day the symbol of doctors and pharmacists.*

* Related reading: *The Zodiac, Key to Man and to the Universe,* Izvor No. 220, Chap. 9.

9 April

Human beings imagine that they are a truly magnificent aspect of nature whereas in reality they often resemble those fat, ugly caterpillars that devour leaves and cause all kinds of damage to trees.* They should withdraw into themselves and begin to reflect and meditate on the necessity of giving up some of their lower inclinations. If they did this, they would set new forces in motion, and after a little while, like caterpillars, they would emerge as dainty, free-flying butterflies, which instead of destroying the foliage simply feed on the nectar of flowers.

Nature has placed signs everywhere to teach disciples and help them to understand the transformations they must work in themselves. Butterflies symbolize the soul that has been set free from all its bonds; this is true resurrection. It is no good thinking that there is a resurrection of the physical body; there is only the awakening of something within which was sleeping and which, after a lengthy work of maturation, emerges into the light.

* Related reading: *Man's Psychic Life: Elements and Structures,* Izvor No. 222, Chap. 13.

10 April

It is always possible to find the means to satisfy a spiritual need precisely because it is spiritual, and because the spirit, which is immense, free and infinite, is not bound by material conditions.

You may be deprived of a title or a rank in society, but no one can deprive you of the feeling that you are a son or daughter of our heavenly Father and of our divine Mother. You can be denied the possession of a few acres of land but no one can deny you the right to contemplate the infinity of the heavens;* and if you succeed in contemplating that immensity, you will experience a fullness that the possession of the whole world could never give you.

---

* Related reading: *Youth: Creators of the Future,* Izvor No. 233, Chap. 9.

11 April

In Genesis we read, *'God breathed into Adam's nostrils the breath of life and man became a living being.'* The life of man began therefore with the breath that God gave him.* And it is still true that the life of every human being begins with a breath. When a child leaves its mother's womb, the first thing it must do in order to become an inhabitant of this earth is to draw breath. It opens its little mouth and screams, and everyone who hears it is glad because this scream tells them that the baby is alive. Thanks to that indrawn breath, the baby's lungs fill with air and begin to function. Conversely, when we say that someone has breathed his last, everybody understands it to mean that he is dead. Breath is the beginning and the end. Life begins with a breath drawn in and ends with a breath expelled.

* Related reading: *The Fruits of the Tree of Life – The Cabbalistic Tradition,* Complete Works, Vol. 32, Chap. 16.

12 April

*T*he peaks of mountains act as antennae that pick up currents from outer space. When the snow and ice begin to melt, the water that runs from them and flows over the surface of the earth, or seeps through the various layers of soil and flows underground, is permeated with these powerful currents.

Waterways are channels of communication between the plains and valleys of the world and its mountaintops. And the mountaintops, like so many mouths, absorb and transform the forces of the cosmos. This is why, when you look at a mountain, you should be aware that it is a transformer of cosmic energy, and that the waters flowing from it are impregnated with this life and communicate it to all the different kingdoms of nature.

13 April

*E*very single thought or feeling is in touch with all the regions and beings in the universe whose vibrations correspond to its own. This explains our joys and sufferings. Someone who drifts into a coarse, bestial way of life unwittingly joins the company of the entities of the lower regions that begin to torment him. If he wants to escape from these regions, he must intensify the vibrations of his cells through prayer, meditation and other spiritual activities such as singing or listening to music.

Abandon all those useless occupations that take up so much of your time and energy for they will bring you nothing but disillusionment, and try to be as closely as possible in touch with the divine world, with your heavenly Father. Get into the habit of repeating as often as possible: 'Lord, may your holy name be blessed for all eternity!' and your anxieties and torment will disappear.

14 April

*T*hose who insist on struggling all alone against their instincts will inevitably become weaker. Yes, because in doing so, they are struggling against themselves and this inner division makes them even more vulnerable. It is very dangerous to struggle against oneself; not only is it impossible to win a complete victory over the enemy within, but one ends up falling apart.

Moral doctrines and religions that constantly preach a fight to the death against evil are ignorant of true psychology. You must learn to overcome, that is true, but not by fighting. How then? By asking other forces to come and fight for you, and these 'other forces' can only be luminous powers that you have nurtured thanks to your love for all that is beautiful, great and divine. Instead of attacking your instincts head on and being floored by them, or becoming completely inhibited, you must confront them with forces of light that will simply proceed to neutralize them.*

* Related reading: *Youth: Creators of the Future,* Izvor No. 233, Chap. 14.

15 April

*O*ur whole life is an endless succession of encounters and contacts with men, women, things and circumstances.* Human beings want to know everything. Why? Because they think that it will be to their advantage. But be careful, the result is often the exact opposite. A fly looks at a spider's web with great curiosity. It wants to find out all about it, never dreaming that the cunning artisan of that magnificent creation is lying in wait for it at the centre of the web. The fly's voyage of exploration ends in a close acquaintance with the spider... but it loses everything in the endeavour. The artist that built this trap is delighted, but that is the end of the fly!

Life is full of spider webs and other snares for the curious and unwary who set off in search of adventure without an instructor or guide.

* Related reading: *New Light on the Gospels,* Izvor No. 217, Chap. 10.

16 April

Why do the lucidity, understanding and clarity of mind of some people continue to grow while in others it is just the opposite, they diminish?* The reason is that the former have a link with universal intelligence; they believe in it and love it, and little by little, it responds to that love and reveals itself to them. Whereas the latter, who refuse to acknowledge its existence, close themselves off from the path of evolution. They rely exclusively on their own intelligence, which is obliged to draw on its own reserves and is soon exhausted.

Those who reject Cosmic Intelligence or deny its existence put limitations on their own mental faculties. Now you are all free to choose which it is to be: the path of all materialistic scientists and philosophers, or the path of the Initiates and great Masters, who constantly receive revelations because they continue to draw on the infinite ocean of Cosmic Intelligence.

* Related reading: *Harmony,* Complete Works, Vol. 6, Chap. 8.

17 April

It is important to understand human nature, to realize once and for all how humans can behave, and how destructive it can be to allow yourself to dwell on people's negative manifestations. For there is a direct link between the things you concern yourself with and your subsequent state of mind. If you continually dwell on other people's faults you will have negative feelings about them, and this will in turn have an adverse effect on you. You must realize that if you dwell constantly on negative things, they will have a detrimental effect on your inner life, and the day will come when even your face reflects those negative feelings that you have nourished.

18 April

Only when a sensitivity to the notions of collectivity and universality has awakened in a person do they truly attain consciousness. This faculty enables them to see into the hearts and souls of other human beings, so that when they cause others to suffer, they feel this suffering in themselves. They understand that whatever they do to others they are doing to themselves. Of course, each human being seems to be alone and apart from all the others, but in reality, there is a spiritual part of ourselves that belongs to the collectivity, that lives in all other creatures and in the cosmos as a whole. When your spiritual dimension is awakened, your being extends throughout the universe and becomes collective.* This means that if you strike someone, it is you yourself who receives the blow through them.

* Related reading: *Love and Sexuality (Part II),* Complete Works, Vol. 15, Chap. 20.

19 April

You feel tired and sad and you have the impression that the whole world is persecuting you. Then night comes, you go to sleep, and in your sleep you take refuge in the other world. The next day when you wake up you feel that everything has changed. What has happened? Quite simply, you managed to flee, and the inner enemies chasing you could not catch you.* This happens automatically, but you can also do it consciously.

Worries, troubles and sorrow are entities that are pursuing you, and the only way to escape is to run to another plane. If the problem lies in your heart go to the intellect; if it is in the intellect, flee to your heart or your soul. If you still feel pursued in your soul, take refuge in the spirit. Nothing and no one can reach you once you are in the spirit.

* Related reading: *Looking into the Invisible,* Izvor No. 228, Chap. 17.

20 April

*T*here is a hierarchy in creation that extends all the way from the earth to the stars. That is to say, the coarser, heavier elements sink to the bottom, whereas the purer, lighter elements rise to the top. This law applies in every sphere, and a disciple who knows this strives to rise as high as possible by means of meditation, contemplation and prayer, so as to capture the subtlest particles of matter with which to build their spiritual bodies. And as these materials are associated with certain energies and entities, the purer the materials the purer and more radiant the energies and entities that come with them. In this way, by replacing the worn-out particles of their body with other, newer particles, a disciple is also introducing more highly evolved visitors into their own psychic being.

21 April

Appearances are often deceptive: behind beauty may lie ugliness; behind wealth, poverty; behind strength, weakness. This is what Hindu philosophy calls maya: false appearances, illusion.*

A wise person is one who has seen through the veil of appearances and found reality. Once they have found this, they have to decide whether or not to pursue their yearnings. Very often, seeing what is in store for them, they will abandon their former ambitions and give up their pursuit of wealth, glory or pleasure. As long as people do not see, as long as they do not understand about maya, they fall into its trap. But once they see things in their true light, they become more prudent.

* Related reading: *Man's Two Natures: Human and Divine*, Izvor No. 213, Chap. 3.

22 *April*

*F*ill a cup or a glass with water, however small, and there in your own home you have all the waters of the world,* for symbolically, magically, even one drop of water puts you in touch with all the rivers, all the oceans. Begin by greeting the water so that it may become even more vibrant and alive. Tell it how much you admire it, how beautiful it is, how you wish that it would grant you something of its purity and transparency. Then you can touch it; dip your fingers into it with the idea that you are touching its etheric body and absorbing its vibrations; that you are imbued with them. If you do this exercise with a sentiment of sacredness, you will feel your body vibrating in harmony with the whole of nature. You will feel lighter and purer and even your brain will function more efficiently.

* Related reading: *The Mysteries of Fire and Water,* Izvor No. 232, Chap. 3.

23 April

The Sun and the Moon with which alchemists work symbolize the masculine and feminine principles. This is why disciples of Initiatic Science know that true alchemy is spiritual alchemy, and that the two principles with which they must work are their will (the Sun) and their imagination (the Moon). By using their will and their imagination, disciples transmute their own matter and become, symbolically speaking, like the Sun and the Moon, that is to say, radiant and pure. *

It is not by chance that astrology says that Aries is ruled by Mars and Taurus by Venus, for it is by working with the Sun and the Moon in order to sublimate their sexual energy (Venus) and the dynamic, active forces of their will (Mars) that alchemists obtain the spiritual powers symbolized by Mercury, the magic agent.

* Related reading: *The Zodiac, Key to Man and to the Universe,* Izvor No. 220, Chap. 9.

24 April

If you really want your love for someone to last, do not be in too much of a rush to get close to them physically, for once the initial passion has abated, you will soon tire of them and begin to see their failings. In order to protect your inspiration you must try to keep a little distance between you.*

When people want to know and experience everything all at once, they soon have no more curiosity about each other. They may even have no desire to see each other again because they have seen and eaten and drunk too much; they are saturated and their beautiful love is all over. They have sacrificed the love that brought them so many blessings, that brought heaven into their lives for the sake of a few minutes of pleasure! Why do they not try to be a little more vigilant? Why are they so quick to deprive themselves of such subtle, poetic sensations?

* Related reading: *Love and Sexuality (Part II),* Complete Works, Vol. 15, Chap. 16.

25 April

When heaven showers blessings on you, guard them closely, for they are very precious, and happiness lies in constant attention to beautiful things and sensitivity to the divine.* When you sense that the spirit, light, has visited you, you must not allow the sensation to evaporate by immediately thinking about other things; keep it alive for as long as possible so that it may sink deeply into you and produce results. In this way, it will leave its mark on you for all eternity.

This must become a habit: instead of always allowing your negative states, your disappointments and animosities to weigh you down, instead of feeding and reinforcing them, leave them aside, forget about them and concentrate on all the good, pure, luminous things that have happened to you.

* Related reading: *The Seeds of Happiness,* Izvor No. 231, Chap. 10.

26 April

When you have to undergo severe trials, instead of complaining about them and protesting, begin by calming yourself. Then think and ask yourself, 'What have the Lord and my friends in heaven planned for me? What is it they want me to gain from it?' Little by little, a light will dawn and you will understand that they want you to become more patient, more resolute and more intelligent. If you do this, not only will you no longer rebel against your trials but you will even be grateful for them, because you will sense that they are enriching. Thanks to this attitude, you will acquire the virtues heaven so urgently wishes for you much more quickly.

27 April

We are all creatures and any creature who refuses to acknowledge that they have a creator is living in the absurd. How can you expect anything intelligent from someone who denies such a simple and obvious fact, that creation and all creatures necessarily have a creator?

When a crime has been committed, the first question people ask is, 'Who did it?' In most cases, the criminal is a long way off by then; he does not remain near his 'handiwork', and yet nobody doubts that the crime had an author. In the same way, if you see an unsigned painting do you say that nobody painted it? Of course not! You simply say that its author is unknown. You do not know who the artist is but you do know that they exist. Then why do some people claim that creation, this magnificent, sublime work of art, has no author? If they prefer, they could say that he is anonymous, but to deny that he exists is the worst possible aberration.*

* Related reading: *Youth: Creators of the Future,* Izvor No. 233, Chap. 2.

28 April

*F*ill your thoughts with light. Concentrate on light; picture it enveloping you and penetrating deep within you. If you do this, not only will you feel protected, shielded from all malevolent influences, but you will also attract to yourself the beneficial forces of the cosmos. You will attract angels who will come and share your work and support you in your efforts. Think of light and imagine it bursting forth from you, streaming throughout space and entering the consciousness of all beings. There is nothing more potent than these exercises with light.*

* Related reading: *Light is a Living Spirit,* Izvor No. 212.

29 April

When a sick person begged Jesus to heal him, why did Jesus ask, *'Do you believe?'* Because if you have faith, it means that you have opened a door through which spiritual forces can enter. Anything you do that involves only your own ability and your own will obeys a purely natural mechanism and is therefore subject to the law of cause and effect.* Whereas as soon as the element of faith comes into it, a door is opened through which other forces, heavenly forces, can enter you and act within you to restore, purify and heal you – sometimes even when you do not quite deserve to be healed!

You could say that faith constrains grace: it opens a door through which grace is obliged to enter. But only on condition, of course, that like the sick man in the Gospel, you beg it to come to you. By calling out to Jesus, the sick man caught his attention, and by his faith, he made it possible for Jesus' power to manifest itself in him.

* Related reading: *Alchemy, Astrology, Magic, Kabbalah – Aspects of esoteric science,* Complete Works, Vol. 4, Chap. 10.

30 April

*T*o perfect oneself is a very difficult undertaking, and when people see how slowly they are progressing, many of them stop trying, while others are so disappointed in themselves that they give way to despair. Well, the former are weak and lazy, and the latter are proud. There is never any reason to despair simply because you realize that you are still a long way from the magnificent image of yourself that you had in mind. Be humble. Say to yourself, 'Old man (or old woman), you have not got there yet, but that does not matter. Keep trying!' The main thing is to keep trying; never to lose your desire to be better.

It does not matter if you fall down, as long as you always make the effort to get up again. Whatever the circumstances of life, the most important thing is to cling to your desire to improve. For there is always room for improvement; the notion of improvement is inseparable from human existence.*

---

* Related reading: *Freedom, the Spirit Triumphant,* Izvor No. 211, Chap. 8.

1 May

For a few minutes every day, try to reach an inner state of silence, a vibrant, living silence in which your soul and spirit are free to speak to their Creator.

If you exercise your ability to concentrate regularly in this way, you will gradually escape – at least for a few minutes at a time – from the mediocrities of everyday life, and the habit will stand you in good stead in moments of difficulty. You will then see how useful it is to be able to detach yourself completely from all your cares and direct your thoughts heavenward.*

* Related reading: *The New Year,* Brochure No. 301, Part 1.

2 May

*T*he letter M, in the form of two peaks separated by a valley, is the expression of a whole science. If you climb to the top of the left-hand peak, for example, you will have to go down into the valley before you can climb the right-hand peak. You have to go down; yes, but if you want to climb the other peak, you must take care not to fall. The two peaks of the letter M are the two poles of a person's psychic life: the self and God. The self, our lower nature, or personality; and God, our higher nature, or individuality.* Our inner forces will be in equilibrium only when we have learned to weave the threads of our lives harmoniously between these two poles.**

* See note and figure on p. 394 and p. 395.

** Related reading: *Man's Two Natures: Human and Divine*, Izvor No. 213, Chap. 2.

3 May

  *T*hose who manage to maintain a certain degree of lucidity in the midst of sexual excitement sometimes realize that they are nourishing entities from the astral world; but the avidity of these creatures is such that they are forced to let them feed on them and drain them of much precious energy. However, most men and women are incapable of analyzing themselves at these moments, and they exclaim, 'Oh, what happiness, what pleasure I felt!' They do not realize that other entities have used them for their own enjoyment. Of course, if their love were truly spiritual, it is they who would gain strength and beauty from it, not others. But this is not the case. As long as their lives are ruled by their passions and instincts, they will continue to be despoiled by inferior entities.*

* Related reading: *Spiritual Alchemy,* Complete Works, Vol. 2, Chap. 9.

4 May

If you want to get the most out of the sunrise, you must prepare for it the evening before. Eat lightly, do not go to bed too late, and do not engage in discussions that will inevitably pursue you the next morning.

When you have learned to watch the sun rising with a mind that is free, you will feel forces of light and joy and resurrection coursing through you. As soon as you begin to breathe and drink in the life of the sun, everything changes: your soul opens, a spring starts to flow within you; the splendour of the dawn enters your being as the pure light in which you are bathed gradually soaks into you. Then you begin to understand the meaning of life, and you yearn to share all these blessings and this great happiness with others.*

* Related reading: *'In Spirit and in Truth'*, Izvor No. 235, Chap. 15.

5 May

Thoughts are very powerful in their own realm, that is to say, on the mental plane. But it takes a long time before they manifest on the physical plane, for they must travel through the different layers of the astral world, which serves as an intermediary between the physical and mental planes. How can we hasten this process? By nurturing feelings and carrying out actions that correspond to our thoughts.

You have all seen in nature how the action of the sun on air creates winds, how the action of the air on water creates ocean waves, and how the action of water on the earth sculpts rock. According to the law of correspondences, water represents the feelings that act upon the earth, the physical body. If great magi have the power to materialize their thoughts, it is because they have learned to work with the intermediaries that allow thoughts to descend to the physical plane.*

* Related reading: *The Powers of Thought,* Izvor No. 224, Chap. 5.

6 May

Cosmic Intelligence has not given human beings the possibility to live on earth forever; it has other plans for them. But it has provided them with a physical body that is capable of lasting for a very long time. The human body is designed in such a way that people could live for hundreds of years if, through their ignorance and their chaotic way of life, they did not do everything in their power to shorten their lives. And because of the unreasonable way in which earlier generations have lived, the heredity of the children born today is already compromised.

If men and women are to have the possibility to once again live much longer (without relying exclusively on the progress of medical science), several generations will have to live wisely and well. One generation would not be enough, for the past is still there and the residue of negative elements cannot be eliminated so quickly. However, if human beings live and behave in accordance with certain rules today, not only will they prepare the ground for later generations, but they will also see some improvements even in this life.*

* Related reading: *On the Art of Teaching (Part III)*, Complete Works, Vol. 29, Chap. 3.

7 May

Because of its great powers of absorption and transmission, water has always had a role to play in magic rites. There are many tales of sorcerers who turned a human being into an animal – a bird, a dog or a horse for instance – after reciting a magic formula over a bowl of water, and sprinkling the water on the victim.

However, the properties of water can also be used for a good purpose. This is why, for example, priests use water to bless the faithful. Since water has the power to retain the currents and influences it receives, it can be a vehicle for the words of blessing.*

* Related reading: *The Mysteries of Fire and Water,* Izvor No. 232, Chap. 8.

8 May

*T*here is no law that forbids you from asserting yourself with others. The only question is how you set about it. A rose asserts itself, but it does so gently, by means of its beauty and its perfume. When the sun shines, it asserts itself, for it makes us take off our coats and jackets. Of course, if you do not wear a hat, you may get sunstroke, but the sun does not use violence, it does not come down from heaven intending to strike you down. It simply says, 'Be careful, my rays are powerful. You must protect yourself, otherwise you will be burnt.' And a rose says, 'Be careful, if you stay close to me I will replace your miasma with my own fragrance.' You have just as much right as the sun and the rose to assert yourself, but it must be by means of light, love, gentleness and beauty.

9 May

A great many people expend all their energy defending this or that insignificant cause – which, as often as not, they soon abandon in favour of something else. But how many do you know who devote their energies to a truly noble idea such as the kingdom of God and his righteousness? Very few. You will say, 'The kingdom of God? But that's a pipe dream! It will never come.' Well, that is not our concern. Our concern is to work towards its realization, for it is the only ideal worth dedicating one's life to; we are not asked to express an opinion about whether it will ever come or not. But one thing is certain: it will never come if nobody makes an effort because they think it is a waste of time and energy.*

* Related reading: *Light is a Living Spirit,* Izvor No. 212, Chap. 9.

10 May

Try to understand the importance of self-mastery. When you learn self-mastery you are the ruler of your own kingdom, and all the treasures and powers of this kingdom are at your disposal. Not only are you then rich and powerful, but you can do a great deal of good for other people; they feel soothed and comforted in your presence. Even the intelligent spirits of the universe come to your assistance, for when they see that you are in full control of yourself, they shower blessings on you, knowing that if they entrust their treasures to you they will not be wasted or lost.*

* Related reading: *Man's Psychic Life: Elements and Structures,* Izvor No. 222, Chap. 5.

11 May

The language of the sun is a universal language that all creatures understand.* It is the language of light, warmth and life. Human beings, animals and plants all understand what the sun is saying. Its very absence or presence is eloquent! Whereas other languages... Do you really believe that the missionaries succeeded in making the language of Christianity understandable to all the Africans and Indians they worked with? No, to many of them it was pure gibberish, and that is only normal. Religion must be built on irrefutable foundations, and who can refute the importance of light, heat and life?

Religions have put too much emphasis on theory or on the external forms of liturgical ceremonies and rites. True religion goes beyond appearances and teaches that human beings must be luminous and full of warmth and life. In other words, they must inwardly possess the intelligence and wisdom that illuminate and solve problems, the selfless love that embellishes, encourages and consoles, and the subtle, spiritual life that makes them active, dynamic and bold in working to establish the kingdom of God on earth.

* Related reading: *A Philosophy of Universality,* Izvor No. 206, Chap. 5.

12 May

If heaven often seems to thwart us by imposing limits and constraints on us, it is in order to awaken within us the will to overcome and free ourselves. Human beings are like gunpowder. If you want gunpowder to explode when you light the fuse, it has to be tightly packed and compressed; if you give it too much room it will just fizzle out. And the same is true of human beings. If their lives are too easy they do no more than sputter; but if they are compressed and made to suffer, something within them rejoices – their spirit, for it is obliged to exert itself and burst its bonds. Yes, you have never realized that while you are suffering and moaning, your spirit rejoices.*

* Related reading: *Freedom, the Spirit Triumphant,* Izvor No. 211, Chap. 7.

13 May

If you are anxious, worried and unhappy, it is because you have not managed to attract any heavenly entities whose presence would enlighten and calm you. You have allowed too many unhealthy, polluted elements to enter your physical body; you have opened the doors of your mental and astral bodies* to impure thoughts and feelings. So do not be surprised if the spirits of light are reluctant to visit you, let alone the Lord, for his dwelling is absolute purity and splendour.

Those who have never worked to purify themselves, and are now sunk in cold, darkness and chaos, need to acknowledge the cause of their distress. They should say, 'The truth is that I have brought it on myself; I have allowed all kinds of evil influences to enter in and now I feel as though heaven has forsaken me.' This is what they should say to themselves for it is the truth; then they should immediately begin to work at their own regeneration.**

* See note and figure on p. 394 and p. 395.

** Related reading: *The Book of Divine Magic,* Izvor No. 226, Chap. 11.

14 May

*H*uman beings currently live in a constant state of tension and agitation, and they think that this is what life is meant to be. They have no objection to spending their days in a flurry of hectic activity. But harmony, beauty and true action are born and manifest themselves in silence. Great works and immortal creations can be accomplished only in the midst of silence.

You must learn to sense the intense life that flows from the heart of this absence of noise and apparent stillness. Silence is the setting for total fulfilment and perfect movement. You should become conscious of this so as to find within yourself the kind of silence from which will spring your most beautiful spiritual creations.*

* Related reading: *The Path of Silence,* Izvor No. 229, Chap. 2.

15 May

You should set aside a few minutes every day in which to create a divine future for yourselves by means of thought. There is not much you can do about the present, but you are all-powerful where the future is concerned, for you are all sons and daughters of God, and the divine spark within you asks for nothing more than to return to the primordial Fire from which it came.

You will say, 'But we are so wretched and have such disabilities! How can we hope for a glorious future?' Well, a remark like that shows that your reasoning is faulty. It is not people who are happy and fulfilled who need to imagine and wish for something better, but those who are unhappy, and they can do so a hundred times more intensely than the others. So, if you feel poor and disinherited, now is the time to use your thoughts to create a future of wealth and splendour.*

* Related reading: *The Seeds of Happiness,* Izvor No. 231, Chap. 21.

16 May

As soon as a new need manifests itself in society, there is always someone who is ready to satisfy that need by giving people what they ask for. The evolution of humankind is thus determined by its needs. Necessity is the mother of invention, they say, and this is true in all spheres of life.

This same law applies on the artistic and spiritual planes. If so few artists create sublime works of art today, it is because there are too few people who are capable of appreciating them. This is only natural – the desires and needs of the few are insufficient to influence creation. And if the kingdom of God has not yet been established on earth, it is because not many people feel the need for it. If great numbers demanded peace and prosperity for the whole world, their demand would be granted.*

* Related reading: *Under the Dove, the Reign of Peace,* Izvor No. 208, Chap. 3.

17 May

It is time the Church stopped talking about the devil as though he were involved in every event and circumstance. Rather than admit that people are turning away from religion because those who represent it are not worthy of their calling, it blames the devil. The devil has even crept into the Church!

How many times have I told you that if you do not have elements within yourselves that attract the devil, and if you are careful not to leave your doors wide open, he is powerless to enter you? Instead of explaining this to people, the Church says that the devil has the power to go in and out wherever he pleases, and no one can stop him. Human beings are so badly built, you see (the Lord cannot have known how to do any better!), that the devil can enter into anyone at will. No, this is quite false. The truth is that no negative power can enter you or even influence you if you do not allow it to do so. This is why Initiatic Science tells us that when it comes to saying 'No!' human beings are as powerful as God Himself.*

* Related reading: *The True Meaning of Christ's Teaching,* Izvor No. 215, Chap. 9.

18 May

A human being represents a tree, with its roots, trunk, branches, leaves, flowers and fruit. All human beings have roots, a trunk and branches, but very few have fruits or flowers, or even leaves, for most of them never see the spring; they are like the forlorn, dark and bare trees of winter. Every human being is potentially capable of flowering, but it takes a great deal of hard work and knowledge, and the sacrifice of much time in order for their flowers to bloom and exhale their perfume, and for their fruit to form. The fruits are a product of the different virtues.*

---

* Related reading: *True Alchemy or the Quest for Perfection,* Izvor No. 221, Chap. 2.

19 May

*P*eople's hearts, intellects and wills rarely work as a team; each one is in the habit of going its own way. The intellect is excited by ideas, but the interests of the heart lie elsewhere; it runs after pleasure and forgets all about the decisions of the intellect. As for the will, it obeys sometimes the one and sometimes the other, or left to its own devices, it does as it pleases.

Most people do not realize that they are full of contradictions and discord; or if they do realize it, they suppose that it is normal and have no idea why it is so. And yet the reason is simple: the three powers within them – the heart, intellect and will – are not pulling together in the same direction. The only way to put an end to this inner conflict is to give yourself a divine ideal and do everything possible to cherish and nourish it until it takes possession of you, until it becomes one with your very being.

20 May

Why haven't you found happiness? Because you look for it on too low a level, in regions that are inimical to it. Happiness is an extremely ethereal, subtle state; it is like a flower that dies when exposed to bad weather. Cosmic Intelligence has placed happiness in the shelter of the higher regions. Yes, Cosmic Intelligence has put its treasures where even noise cannot penetrate.

To reach these higher regions, your soul must vibrate on a higher frequency; you must wrest yourself from the level of your ordinary passions and their great fluctuations. A disciple can rise to the level on which Cosmic Intelligence has placed happiness only by introducing silence into their soul.*

* Related reading: *The Seeds of Happiness,* Izvor No. 231, Chap. 13.

21 May

In everyday life, it is perfectly reasonable and right for everybody to express and defend their own point of view. As long as people have no knowledge of the eternal truths of Initiatic Science, they need to exercise their wits, to argue and discuss, to fight and be at each other's throats. All that is normal. It is even possible that in crossing swords and striking sparks, they may end up coming closer to the truth.

Yes, but once you are in an initiatic school and are learning about the great laws of the cosmos, why do you still argue and criticize and try to impose your personal views on others? In society, diverging opinions and debate are fine; we need many thinkers, scientists and teachers to analyze, theorize and discuss ideas, but now that you have found the truth of Initiatic Science, you no longer need to waste your time in discussion. You only need to put these truths into practice.*

* Related reading: *Truth, Fruit of Wisdom and Love,* Izvor No. 234, Chap. 10.

22 May

If everything you do is ruled by the law of justice, you are like the grocer who sells a pound of cherries and weighs them to be sure that you do not get one cherry too many. With justice of this kind, the grocer will soon have no more customers. You should always give more than you owe, for in this way you make people happy and win their friendship.

Justice was useful in former times when human beings were not ready to accept the teachings of Christ, the teaching of love. The Old Testament speaks only about justice: '*an eye for an eye, a tooth for a tooth*'; but to follow this rule today would mean a great loss. The invisible world would say, 'Since you always behave with justice, justice will be your lot for eternity', and this would be really terrible. But if you work according to the law of love, then you will meet with love. The law of justice is a necessary basis for moral conduct, but it is not sufficient for the establishment on earth of the kingdom of God 'and his justice' – for divine justice is not human justice. Love will always transcend justice.*

* Related reading: *Man, Master of his Destiny,* Izvor No. 202, Chap. 4.

23 May

When God told the first men and women to *'fill the earth and subdue it'*, He was referring to a very specific 'earth': their head. What goes on in a person's head is a reflection of what is happening on earth, and vice versa; and if war is always present on earth, it is because there is war in people's heads. Even the five continents – Africa, Asia, America, Australasia and Europe – are represented in our heads. The occiput, for example, represents Africa.

The ideal of a disciple is to have a magnificently shaped head. A master can tell from the structure of a person's head what kind of 'earth' they live in.*

* Related reading: *Under the Dove, the Reign of Peace,* Izvor No. 208, Chap. 9.

24 May

Centuries ago, human beings decided that it was best to be cold, stiff and uncommunicative in public. This was considered to be the epitome of wisdom! It was bad form to be enthusiastic, friendly and vibrantly alive. This is why thousands of people today are without light, warmth or joy; they have no idea how unpleasant they are, and others do not wish to be around them. Well, it is time to change this attitude. From now on, you must cultivate life. Work to enhance the intensity of your life, to raise the vibrations of your whole being to a higher frequency so as to project rays of life and light into the world around you.*

* Related reading: *On the Art of Teaching (Part III)*, Complete Works, Vol. 29, Chap. 6.

For as long as the human race has existed, it has been faced with the same questions, so our Teaching does not present you with new topics. What is new is the point of view. Take the universal question of love for instance: it is the favourite subject of poets, and every novel, play or film has to have a love story in one form or another. People want to know how lovers meet, how they fall in love, how they part ways... The names, times and places change, but the story is always the same – it is extraordinary to see that human beings never tire of hearing or reading the same thing over and over again.

Love is also the essential question for a spiritual master; but there is a great difference in his way of understanding and living it. He will tell you, 'If you fail to find love, it is because you look for it only in a man or woman. Love is disseminated in every part of the universe from the stones to the stars. This is where you must seek it, contemplate it, eat and breathe it. Only once you find the love that permeates every creature and the whole of creation can you say that you have truly found love, and then will you dwell in the fullness of love.'

26 May

It is possible, by means of thought, to get all the elements we need from the universe, and to reach all the beings we wish to contact. Thanks to the law of affinity, our thoughts go directly to the elements and beings we are seeking. When you think of one particular person amongst all the billions of individuals on earth, your thought unerringly reaches him or her, as though it were programmed to home in on that person and on no other. So from now on, when you need an element or want to reach a being somewhere in the universe, think of them without worrying about where they might be. As long as your thoughts are intense, they will fly straight to their target.*

* Related reading: *The Laughter of a Sage,* Izvor No. 243, Chap. 12.

27 May

*T*he most profound revelations about life are given to us by the sun. So if you genuinely want to learn, turn to the sun. Look at it and ask it to explain its light and heat.

But you should also concentrate on the thought that you yourself are in the sun, for this is the reality: your higher Self is in the sun. The sun is its home. Then, when you sense that you have succeeded in identifying with your higher Self in the sun, glance down at the being on earth who is also you. In this way, you establish a bond between yourself and the sun; a bond that is like a circle of magic, a current that you will experience as a salutary tide of purification and illumination.*

* Related reading: *Toward a Solar Civilization,* Izvor No. 201, Chap. 8.

28 May

Nothing is more precious than to be visited by the Holy Spirit. Its coming is like a bolt of heavenly lightning. There is nothing more sublime or more meaningful. However, this celestial lightning does not immediately make those who receive it all-knowing, all-powerful and perfect. No, but it does make it possible for them to become so; it is up to them to work with the fire they have received.

Unfortunately, people can also lose this grace, and to lose the Holy Spirit is the most terrible loss any human being can suffer. Many spiritualists, mystics and initiates who once possessed this fire have lost it in one way or another. Some of them managed to recover it, but at the price of what suffering, labours and tears of repentance! They had to plead with the utmost humility for a long time before the fire agreed to return to them. But once the heavenly fire returns to someone, it clings to them so stubbornly and thrusts its roots so deeply into their being that it can no longer be torn from them. From that moment on, it guides, controls and orientates the person's life.*

* Related reading: *The Splendour of Tiphareth – The Yoga of the Sun,* Complete Works, Vol. 10, Chap. 21.

On the grand scale of joy – for yes, joy, like many other states of mind, exists on a scale that has different degrees or levels – one level of joy comes from eating, another from breathing, another from walking, another from reading, or singing, or kissing your beloved, and so on. On this scale, the joy that tops all others is the joy that comes from being one with the Creator.

The Creator has given all creatures the possibility of experiencing an infinite range of joys, but He has reserved the supreme joy for those who achieve union with Him. Once a human being has achieved this union, they are able to radiate the light of the Godhead, to manifest it consciously for the benefit of the whole world, and to help others and show them the way. This represents the highest degree on the scale of joy.

30 May

*S*uppose two people decide to marry or form a partnership: are they concerned about whether their affinity extends to the realm of ideas?* No, they are drawn to each other and that is enough, they look no further.

Well, a mutual attraction and liking is all very well, but as time goes on, there will be days when it is important to agree on the level of ideas. And as they cannot see eye to eye, a state of conflict develops and before long, their initial affection vanishes and is transformed into an implacable hatred. This is always the outcome, whether in love or friendship, when one neglects the question of intellectual compatibility.

* Related reading: *Life Force,* Complete Works, Vol. 5, Chap. 11.

31 May

It is fine to want to be free, but not by just any means. Many people do everything possible to escape their obligations, run away from their duty, and sever their ties to others, thinking that they will then be free. No, that is not the way to be free.

True liberation consists in paying one's debts, not in abandoning one's wife and children, leaving one's job and dropping out of society... or even of life itself by committing suicide!* This would be like eating a hearty meal in a restaurant and then trying to slip out without paying the bill. It is dishonest. To behave in this way shows a lack of all sense of responsibility, and it will not be countenanced by the spirits of light who watch over us. In fact, those who try to free themselves in this way inevitably meet all kinds of new problems and constraints to teach them that they are mistaken. They have jumped from the frying pan into the fire! There can be no liberation until we have paid all our debts and wiped out our karma. We must all try to free ourselves, but only by means that are in harmony with divine law.

* Related reading: *The Tree of the Knowledge of Good and Evil,* Izvor No. 210, Chap. 8.

1 June

We must learn to make use of every opportunity we are given to transcend the mediocrity of life. The silence of the night and the starry sky offer us the best conditions to forget about human affairs for a while and think of other worlds where more evolved beings live in harmony and splendour. All our concerns mean nothing to them; they are insignificant events. You will say, 'What do you mean, insignificant events? Famine, massacres and disasters are terrible!' Yes, they are terrible, but in the eyes of Cosmic Intelligence, they do not merit much attention. For Cosmic Intelligence, only the events of the soul and the spirit are important.*

* Related reading: *The Path of Silence, Izvor No. 229,* Chap. 13.

2 June

*H*uman beings continually transgress divine laws, and as they do not immediately notice the damage occurring inside them, they imagine that they can carry on with impunity. The thing is, when worms or termites get into the beams of a house, there are no visible signs of their destructive endeavours at first – until one day the house collapses. So, it is very poor reasoning to rely on immediate results.

How many times have people complained to me, 'Master, I have been doing spiritual work for years and I don't see any results!' This too is poor reasoning. For the work carried out by the luminous spirits in humans is not immediately visible or tangible either. Chemistry gives us an illustration of this process of transformation. Drop by drop, you pour acid into an alkaline solution – there is no reaction. And then you add just one more drop... and all of a sudden the solution changes colour.* So, we must not imagine that nothing is happening simply because it takes a long time before we see any reaction.

* Related reading: *Christmas and Easter in the Initiatic Tradition,* Izvor No. 209, Chap. 5.

3 June

You must constantly think to re-establish the link within you between the world below and the world on high. What is a magic wand? It is a rod that connects the two worlds. A magus who does not possess this rod internally cannot activate the forces of nature within him, nor accomplish a feat of magic. Even if he holds the wand, it remains external to him because he has not understood that a true magic wand is a live connection that allows the current to flow between earth and heaven, just like when you insert a plug into a socket. The role of a magic wand is to provide a connection so that energies can flow from one world to the other.

There is a power station, God, who provides the current, and in order for a lamp to light up, we must plug it in. Well, a magic wand is in fact the plug. So, when a magus possesses this plug in his head and in his heart, and then holds in his hand a magic wand, which represents this plug on the physical plane, he can transfer forces from the divine world to the physical world. This is the symbol of the magic wand.*

* Related reading: *The Fruits of the Tree of Life – The Cabbalistic Tradition,* Complete Works, Vol. 32, Chap. 21.

4 June

Disciples of an Initiatic School are like orchards where all sorts of fruit trees grow. The divine gardeners, those intelligent and luminous spirits of nature, come to visit and say, 'Oh, this watermelon, this cantaloupe, this peach... what wonderful fruits! Come on, let's taste them!' Yes, when they see a being who is finally awakening to the spiritual life, they tend to them, delighting in everything luminous that radiates and emanates from them. So it is that all women and men are visited by gardeners from heaven.

Some will say, 'But I have nothing to give, I am not an orchard, how can anyone come and get anything from me?'* In reality, there is always some useful element to extract, even from poisonous plants, if only to make medicine. This is why, even if they do not realize it, humans are visited by creatures from the other world that come to gather and make use of the elements they emanate.

* Related reading: *Toward a Solar Civilization,* Izvor No. 201, Chap. 2.

5 June

We see people all over the world doing everything they can to move up in rank. They know that each time they climb a rung on the ladder, they will be paid more respect, earn more money, have more responsibilities and be in charge of more people. Yes, a change in position! There is a great lesson in this matter; everyone knows it, sees it and tries to put it into practice. Unfortunately, only a very small minority of beings have understood that we must make the same effort to rise in rank internally in order to gain more prestige and thus be listened to and obeyed by the population of cells within us that want only to do as they please.

Just look at a police officer directing traffic in the street: everyone obeys him. He says, 'Move along', and even the greatest professors move ahead. He may not be educated himself, but his uniform and small baton suffice. The same thing happens in you: if you wear certain 'clothing', certain 'badges', your cells, which are your subjects, your subordinates, are impressed and they obey you.*

---

* Related reading: *What is a Spiritual Master?* Izvor No. 207, Chap. 3.

6 June

Look how on the physical plane, human beings have improved the tools and devices they use to work and defend themselves: pneumatic drills have replaced picks and axes, vacuum cleaners have replaced brooms... there are also tanks, canons, rockets and so on. But on the spiritual plane, people remain poor and defenceless. And yet there are all sorts of means and weapons: a talisman, a pentacle, the image of a saint, a cross and so forth. Everything that has been found on the physical plane has its equivalent on the spiritual plane. Clothes, for example, which are a protection against the cold and against blows, represent a kind of talisman.

On the spiritual plane, the aura serves this purpose. The aura is one of the best forms of protection, but anything can be used to protect oneself, even a look, a smile or a wave of the hand. We use our hands so often to protect ourselves physically! We must also learn to use them to protect ourselves on the spiritual plane.*

* Related reading: *Man's Subtle Bodies and Centres,* Izvor No. 219, Chap. 2.

7 June

When you see a person suffering, you do not know whether their suffering is inflicted by divine justice or whether they have freely consented to it. How can we tell if someone is being punished, or if they have chosen to sacrifice themselves? Many say, 'This man is good and honest so if he is suffering, it must be because he made mistakes in a past incarnation, which he must now fix', and they do nothing to help him. But perhaps they are mistaken.

It is extraordinary – when people suffer, they obviously think that this suffering is unfair, that they do not deserve it, whereas they always find a way to justify the suffering of others. Well, from now on, you must do the opposite: when you are suffering, tell yourself that this suffering is undoubtedly justified, but when others are suffering, think that they are perhaps not guilty and that they deserve your help and understanding. This way of doing things will help you enormously to grow.

*M*aster Peter Deunov gave the following rule: 'Make goodness the foundation of your life, justice your measure, wisdom your shield, love your delight and truth your light'.

If we reflect on the meaning of this precept, we will find it remarkably accurate. Goodness is the one solid base upon which a building can rest. Even if this building is beautiful and intelligent, it will collapse if goodness does not support it. Justice is a quality of measurement; as shown by the scales that symbolize it, to be just requires knowing how to keep a balance at all times: adding a little on one side, removing a little from the other. Wisdom is a shield with which we can protect ourselves against external and internal enemies who threaten us. Life seems insipid without love; even if we have everything – riches, knowledge and fame – without love, we would have no zest for life. Truth is the light that illuminates our path; without it, we are in darkness and we go astray.*

* Related reading: *Life with the Master Peter Deunov. Autobiographical Reflections 2.*

9 June

During the meditations, get into the habit of concentrating on the celestial light, so as to attract it and draw it into you; there, it will gradually replace all the old, soiled and worn-out material with new particles of the utmost purity. And once you have drawn the light into you, you must then train yourself to send it out to the whole world in order to help human beings.

Many people believe they are justified in giving way to a life of selfishness and mediocrity, on the pretext that they have no special talents or qualities. No, no one can be justified in doing this. Even if you are the most deprived being in every respect, you can do this work with the light, and in so doing achieve something more important and more useful than anything that can be accomplished by the most capable people in any other field. Even the most destitute being can acquire this higher state of consciousness in order to work to attract the light and send it out to all humanity.*

* Related reading: *Light is a Living Spirit,* Izvor No. 212, Chap. 9.

10 June

*T*he annals of Initiatic Science mention that many humanities have already disappeared, and that some of them had a culture far more advanced than ours.* They reason they disappeared is because of the lower nature's tendency to push beings to want to dominate and enslave everything through violence. And the fact that we see these tendencies increasingly on the rise in our societies is a very bad sign for the future of humankind.

This is why it is urgent that human beings learn to put the impulses of their lower nature at the service of their higher nature. Otherwise, what is one humanity more or less to Cosmic Intelligence, which lives in eternity? So many others have disappeared, that if this one were also to disappear of its own doing, it would not make much difference to Cosmic Intelligence: it would prepare a new one with the few people remaining, It is up to us not to destroy ourselves. If we are bent on self-destruction, Cosmic Intelligence will remain impassive and leave us to it.

* Related reading: *A New Dawn: Society and Politics in the Light of Initiatic Science (Part I),* Complete Works, Vol. 25, Chap. 8, Part 3.

11 June

People are complaining more and more about pollution: the earth, water, air, everything is polluted – and plants, fish, birds and humans are increasingly threatened with each passing day. Remedies are hard to find, and even if they were found, they would affect only the exterior side of things, the physical plane, and that is not enough.

For toxic products, exhaust fumes and smoke are everywhere in the psychic world as well, and they are killing humankind. If so many people are sick nowadays, it is not due solely to the pollution in the air, water and food. No! If the psychic atmosphere were not so polluted, human beings would be able to neutralize all external poisons. The trouble lies first on the inside. When human beings live in harmony, the forces they possess inside react and reject impurities, even those on the physical plane, which is how the body is able to defend itself. We are vulnerable first and foremost on the psychic plane, and little by little, this weakness spreads to the physical plane.*

* Related reading: *The Powers of Thought,* Izvor No. 224, Chap. 3.

12 June

We need to be in contact with this luminous, warm, life-giving power that is the sun in order to understand it and receive it. But in order to come into contact with the sun, our mind must not be preoccupied with thoughts that might lead it to wander; our heart must not be occupied left and right, but focused on the sun; and finally, we must be sufficiently prepared physically to remain before the sun while staying vigilant.

So there are three conditions: free your thoughts, free your heart, and be physically well disposed. Then, we can concentrate so as to receive the vibrant rays of the sun that are powerful and rich, and imagine that we are storing them up in the cells of our brain, but especially in our solar plexus. For the solar plexus is like a reservoir that is able to house these energies, which we can then draw upon as and when we need them.

*T*here are beings who come into this world totally free of faults and passions; and these beings are predestined for great work. Of course, due to heredity, they are very rare, for there are so few families on earth that are perfectly pure and able to provide a perfect body for the luminous spirits that wish to come and incarnate. Even the greatest initiates are obliged to work on their body for many years to correct certain flaws and defects. Even if their spirit helps the mother during gestation, working with her to gather the best materials, they cannot prevent a few hereditary defects from creeping in.

This is why those who wish to raise a family must never forget that they have tremendous opportunities to help the spirits of light to incarnate in the most favourable conditions. And what gratitude they will then receive from these spirits who will become their children! At the moment, we do not help them very much, so although they come from heavenly regions, they are forced to bear heavy burdens.

14 June

Devote at least a few minutes each day to introducing harmony within you. Close your eyes while making an effort to free your mind of everyday worries, and direct your thoughts towards the heights, towards the sources of life that flood the entire universe.

When you feel that you have stopped the flow of thoughts and images passing through you, say the words 'thank you' inwardly. These are the simplest words, yet they relieve all tension because in giving thanks, you attune yourself with heaven; you come out of the narrow circle of yourself and penetrate the peace of cosmic consciousness. Remain in this state as long as you can, and when you come back to yourself, you will feel that new and very precious elements have made their way into you: serenity, lucidity and strength.*

* Related reading: *The Path of Silence,* Izvor No. 229, Chap. 12.

15 June

*T*he most powerful force of all forces that Hermes Trismegistus speaks of in the Emerald Tablet is sexual force. For what other force in the universe can compare to it? What other force has the power to create life? And if we go deeper into what Hermes Trismegistus says about it – 'The sun is its father' – we understand that sexual energy is of the same nature as solar energy, that it is imbued with the holiness, light and life of the sun, and that it can be used for wonderful creations.

Unfortunately, human beings have become so debased that the act by which a man fertilizes a woman no longer has anything solar about it. But it must become so again. And not just this act; all the actions of our daily life must become solar again, that is to say luminous, warm and vivifying.*

* Related reading: *Sexual Force or the Winged Dragon,* Izvor No. 205.

*T*hose who work with the cold (wisdom) must also work with heat (love) and vice versa. By passing from one pole to the other, they maintain their equilibrium and discover the life that lies in this back and forth movement. Those who remain forever in the cold or in the heat do not evolve; it is all over for them.

How do you go about cooking your vegetables? You place the pot on the stove, but after a while, you remove it. Why do you not let everything burn? Because you are wise. If you feel love for someone, that is good; but wisdom tells you not to go too far because it is not advisable. If you feel heat rising within you with regard to someone, do not leave the pot on the stove! Heat (love) is welcome, but it must be followed by a bit of cooling: wisdom.*

* Related reading: *The Zodiac, Key to Man and to the Universe,* Izvor No. 220, Chap. 7.

17 June

When you concentrate on the highest ideal, God Himself, who is beauty, light, purity and absolute power, a magical phenomenon occurs: an entire network of energies is woven between the forces of your being and this ideal.

This ideal activates hidden forces within our being; it awakens them and draws them to itself. There is a polarization between our being and the ideal that not only serves as a means of comparison, a yardstick, a model, a sample, but it also serves as a magical element that activates the forces of consciousness, of self-consciousness. An ideal influences the mind so that it learns to distinguish, discern, classify and recognize what is perfect. An ideal awakens warmth and love in the heart; and through an ideal, the will is stimulated and energized. Thus, your high ideal brings harmony and attunes all your cells to God Himself.*

* Related reading: *The High Ideal,* Brochure No. 307.

18 June

Why do you always expect others to start to work to make the world a better place? Why don't you get started yourself? You wait for others to make the effort, but others do the same as you: they are waiting for you to get to work, and this can go on indefinitely.

What willpower, what faith it takes to do good in a world where everything is going awry! But this is precisely why it is so commendable. In favourable circumstances, it is too easy to believe in good and to do good – everything is simple and pleasant. No, no, it is now, as the situation worsens that it is worthwhile continuing without letting yourself be influenced by the conditions. We must learn to count on the powers of the spirit; this is the sign of a truly spiritual person. Of course, many people give lip service to being spiritual, but when faced with the slightest obstacle they immediately fall apart. Despite the conditions, despite the storm, truly spiritual people always strive to awaken the powers of the will, of goodness and of light.

19 June

*T*rue morality is based on laws established by Cosmic Intelligence, it is not a human invention that varies according to time and place. If you are caught breaking human laws, or transgressing certain codes of conduct or limits, you must pay; but if you are not caught, nature will not come to punish you since you have transgressed only human morals. Whereas if you transgress the laws of nature, you will not get away with it. Even if humans bow to you and crown you in glory, nature will punish you: you will be troubled and physically or psychically unwell.

Obviously, this is no reason to break human laws, not at all. It is said, *'Give to Caesar the things that are Caesar's, and to God the things that are God's'*, which is to say respect the laws of the land, the laws of humans, but above all, respect the laws of God.*

---

* Related reading: *The Key to the Problems of Existence,* Complete Works, Vol. 11, Chap. 14.

20 June

Depending on how you consider beings or things, you either enhance them or detract from them. Suppose you have to take some medicine: it is very much up to you whether you reduce its potency or heighten it. If you do not really believe in it, it will still work, of course, but a little less so than if you had put all your faith in it.

By the way in which you consider things, you introduce something of yourself into them that is likely to transform them. However, human beings are generally content to take things as they are – people are passive, they are not creators and that is a shame! If they were conscious, they could add so many beneficial elements to everything they do!

21 June

*D*o you want to know what will happen to you if you indulge in sensuality? Look at a drunkard who is completely befuddled and dazed: you will become exactly like him. 'Oh no', you will say, 'I know men who change mistresses all the time, and yet they read, study and do wonderful work.' Yes, of course, sensuality is compatible with certain intellectual or artistic faculties, but when it comes to reaching the heavenly regions, of carrying out spiritual work, they will find that they no longer possess the necessary elements, and moreover, they have no desire to elevate themselves.

Look at bees that have gorged themselves on honey: they are too heavy and can no longer fly. It is the same with men and women who have not learned to control their sexual instincts – they can continue to do all sorts of work, but they can no longer fly. The heavenly regions are forbidden to them.

22 June

*H*uman beings receive instruction for all kinds of activities, but they are never taught what true work is. True work is to strive towards the perfection of the Lord. We have been given all the means to achieve this: a will, heart, intellect, soul and spirit.

Unfortunately, humans are capable of making use of everything nature has given them – their eyes, mouth, hands, feet and sexual organs – to engage in madness and self-destruction, but when it comes to doing sublime work, they just sit there and do nothing. From now on, we must mobilize everything that nature has given us in the way of organs and faculties to achieve perfection and to become, at last, true sons and daughters of God.*

* Related reading: *The Powers of Thought,* Izvor No. 224, Chap. 1.

23 June

Jesus is often portrayed as the 'good shepherd' who protects his flock. But human beings are also shepherds for their cells, which they must protect from the wolves always trying to breach the sheepfold, that is to say, germs and viruses, but also the evil spirits and undesirables that constantly assail them.

When people do not apply the great truths of the divine world or live in harmony with the rules of living nature, their body weakens. This is why they must link themselves to the light, and learn to project it into their cells to drive out the 'wolves' from within. This is Christ's teaching. Loving Jesus and preaching as we have been doing for the past two thousand years is of no use; this is the external side of religion, the easy side. The true religion of Christ means to place all our trust in the power of light, in the power of the spirit that revitalizes, strengthens and liberates. Then, yes, humans become good shepherds to their flock.

24 June

Solitude is a state of consciousness that everyone, even the greatest Initiates, must go through at some point in their existence. It is a dark and empty space in which we no longer know where we are or where we are going. Christ himself passed through this dark and deserted space when he said, *'My God, why have You forsaken me?'* Everyone will one day experience this indescribable solitude. Why? Because it is when we feel alone and abandoned that we develop true faith, hope and love, not when we are happy, satisfied and surrounded by friends.

In reality, no one is ever abandoned in the true sense of the word, each of us is surrounded by spirits and entities of all kinds. When we go through certain ordeals we may feel alone and abandoned, but in reality, no, solitude does not exist. That is why there is no other way to get through this inner state than to rely on the Being who sustains all the worlds and all the stars; we must believe in this immortal Being, love Him and hope in Him.*

* Related reading: *Golden Rules for Everyday Life,* Izvor No. 227, Chap. 94.

25 June

Sometimes it is useful to go on a retreat for a few days in order to escape from our worries and cares. You will say, 'But if we try to escape from our problems we will never solve them!' Ah, this is just where you are mistaken. It is not because you obsess about your problems that you are actually solving them; quite the contrary – often, you nurture them. Try to set your problems aside and soon after, thanks to your inner work, you will receive a light that will allow you to find the solution.

We often say 'let me sleep on it'. Yes, because while we are asleep, we forget about everything and work goes on in our subconscious that then allows us to see more clearly and find solutions. So, why not do the same thing consciously from time to time?

26 June

There are people who, believing they see the Lord's reputation under attack everywhere they look, mobilize to defend Him. As if the Lord were so weak that He needed to be defended! Well, this is what they believe. And so they condemn, they persecute and they slaughter. If they were honest, they would ask the Lord for His opinion and they would hear the Lord, who is Love, reply, 'Do not worry about this, it is not your concern. If they are really that wicked, they will destroy themselves.' But in truth, do you really think that it is the Lord they are defending? No, what they are defending are their own affairs, their own prestige, influence and power, that is all. What hypocrisy! When we truly want to defend the Lord, we must show patience and love as He does.*

* Related reading: *The Faith That Moves Mountains,* Izvor No. 238, Chap. 6.

27 June

*A*ll Initiations, past as well as present, teach just one thing: how to achieve the union of spirit and matter.* Yes, just one thing, the union, the fusion of spirit and matter, of human beings and their Creator; however, the explanations, presentations and aspects are infinite. For a wealth of knowledge must be acquired to achieve this fusion. All the sciences serve a single goal: to unite with the Godhead, to become one with the First Cause.

Human beings are always searching for who knows what... But there is no need to search, everything is clear: there is nothing to seek other than union with God, and all the discoveries in the various fields of science should contribute exclusively to achieving this union.

* Related reading: *New Light on the Gospels,* Izvor No. 217, Chap. 1.

28 June

When you are in love, are you in any doubt about it? No. Yet you cannot see your love, you cannot touch it, it is something intangible. When you have an opinion, do you see it? No. And yet you are sometimes ready to fight and die for it. When you say, 'In my soul and conscience, I condemn this man', you are also condemning him in the name of something you cannot see. How is it that you attach so much importance to this invisible soul and conscience? Without realizing it, the whole world believes in invisible, intangible things: everyone feels, loves, suffers, cries and rejoices for reasons that cannot be seen... and then they claim they believe only in what they can see and touch. How contradictory!*

* Related reading: *On the Art of Teaching (Part III)*, Complete Works, Vol. 29, Chap. 6.

29 June

You will never be a true economist until you understand that economy first and foremost involves not wasting the strength and qualities bestowed upon you by heaven. Yes, economy therefore begins with wisdom, moderation and care. Nowadays, the world is crawling with economists – they are everywhere! But humanity will never be able to find happiness with these economists because they consider strictly the material side of life and of problems.

First of all, economy must begin on high, on the psychic plane: in our thoughts, feelings, looks, words and behaviour, so as not to cause disorder in the invisible world. For the invisible world is populated, organized and governed by laws, and if we unconsciously trigger mechanisms, if we disturb entities or transgress the laws, we suffer the consequences... until such time as we understand what true economy is.*

* Related reading: *Under the Dove, the Reign of Peace,* Izvor No. 208, Chap. 7.

30 June

When you want to meditate, do not try to concentrate abruptly, otherwise your brain will seize up. Our mind likes to wander and roam, which is why you must start by giving it free rein for a while. This instrument, known as the brain, must be put to work very gently, just as you would let the engine of your car warm up before driving off.

Begin by putting yourself in a state of peace and harmony then gently lead your thought in the direction you want it to go: after a while, it will be at your disposal and will obey you. Whereas if you want to dominate and control it abruptly, it will retaliate, rear up and even knock you down. You must be very clever and very diplomatic with your thought, which is difficult. But when you know how to dominate it, you are able to concentrate and do such powerful work that it does not stop all day long; it continues in the same direction without further intervention on your part.*

* Related reading: *Meditation,* Brochure No. 302.

1 July

The Book of Genesis tells how one night, Jacob slept with his head upon a stone and while he slept, he dreamed that he saw a ladder linking heaven and earth upon which angels were going up and down. Jacob's dream was a revelation of the celestial hierarchy that extends from the earth to heaven and which is represented in the Cabbalah as the Sephirotic Tree, the Tree of Life*.

A knowledge of this hierarchy is indispensable to our inner lives. If humans understand that everything, from the stones of the earth to God himself, is linked hierarchically, and if they keep this idea of an ordered structure in the universe constantly in mind, they will be obliged to behave accordingly, because they will realize that everything must fit into its proper place in the universal harmony. If most human beings today are so troubled, if they have lost all understanding of the meaning of life, it is because they fail to respect the true hierarchy established by Cosmic Intelligence since time immemorial.**

* See note and figure on p. 396-399.

** Related reading: *A New Dawn: Society and Politics in the Light of Initiatic Science (Part I),* Complete Works, Vol. 25, Chap. 8.

2 July

Get into the habit of watching and listening to the life of nature: to stones, plants and animals, and above all, to the four elements in whatever form they may appear – rocks, sand, rain, snow, wind, sun, stars and so on.

There are so many things to observe and interpret! Just think of the different shapes and colours of clouds – all the cavalcades, battles and fiestas we see are the work of the spirits of air. For there is a life on high that manifests itself in a multitude of forms: faces, birds, flocks of sheep, landscapes... There are even forms of writing that we do not yet know how to decipher. But that is not an issue; what is essential is to consciously let all these images sink in.*

* Related reading: *The Mysteries of Fire and Water,* Izvor No. 232, Chap. 18.

3 July

Not only is it important to wash one's feet, but it is also important to know how to do so. This is because, firstly, it is through our feet that we are continually in contact with the ground, from which they pick up influences and currents. We should therefore prepare them to be good receivers. Secondly, our feet are connected to our whole body, and particularly to our nervous system: the solar plexus and the brain.

Our head and feet are the two poles of our body: our head puts us in contact with the heavens and our feet, with the earth. If we want to establish good communications between our head and feet, we must do some work with our feet. We must touch them consciously and lovingly, and talk to them so that they too may have a part in our spiritual activity. Everything is of importance, for everything must contribute to advancing our evolution.*

* Related reading: *Life with the Master Peter Deunov. Autobiographical Reflections 2.*

*P*eople are stingy but not economical. It is not necessarily selfish to be economical, just as it is not necessarily generous to be extravagant. You must learn to make the distinction. Those who squander their energies and throw money out of the window are said to be generous. No, they are rash, vain, stupid, or whatever you like, but not generous. If you want to practise generosity, you must learn the art of saving, for what will you have to share with others if you squander all your wealth? To be economical is to spend where and when you need to, and as much as you need to but no more.

5 July

The sun's rays give life to each object or being they fall on. Even stones need the life they receive from the sun, for although stones are inanimate, they are alive. Life is even more apparent in plants, which grow and multiply thanks to sunlight. In animals, the sun's rays are transformed not only into vitality, but also into sensitivity. Yes, it is thanks to the sun's rays that animals begin to feel suffering or joy. Finally, in humans, the sun's rays are transformed into intelligence, for it is from the human realm upwards that light begins to find the welcome it needs to manifest itself as thought.

The spirit that speaks through the mouth of a person is an emanation of solar light. It is light that thinks, speaks, sings and creates. As light gradually works its way into a human soul, it is reflected in the form of intelligence, love, beauty, nobility and strength.*

* Related reading: *Light is a Living Spirit,* Izvor No. 212, Chap. 2.

6 July

At each hour, minute and second of the day, you determine your own future. If at a given moment you choose light, from that moment on, it is decided; you are on the road to eternal glory. If a moment later you choose darkness, there again it is decided, and you are on the way to hell. You decide your own orientation at each moment, but it will be centuries before your decision takes effect on the physical plane. Although in reality nothing has changed here, there is a change of direction on high.

When a signalman activates a switch, the train runs onto a different track, and this is what a human being does every day, sometimes a hundred or a thousand times a day. At one moment they are heading straight for hell; the next moment they are on the way to heaven. On the physical plane there is no visible difference, but each change of direction is recorded. If you want your orientation to be stable, you must keep unswervingly to the same track and, in this way, that orientation will set to work and shape your life once and for all.*

* Related reading: *Cosmic Moral Laws,* Complete Works, Vol. 12, Chap. 16.

7 July

Human beings have an innate tendency to avoid exerting themselves. They always try to get others – people, animals or machines – to do their work for them. In doing so, they weaken themselves and lose their own faculties.

Those who want to be strong and intelligent, and capable of standing up to whatever comes should get into the habit of making an effort. It is possible today to acquire all kinds of things without exerting oneself at all, but what will this lead to? People will be outwardly satisfied and that is all; inwardly they will be empty, hollow. It is the efforts they make that keep humans alive and stalwart.*

* Related reading: *The Seeds of Happiness,* Izvor No. 231, Chap. 4.

8 July

Knowledge of the law of karma should not be an excuse for indifference to the sufferings of others. Unfortunately, instead of thinking about all those who suffer, and deciding to do something for them, many so-called spiritual people who have heard of this law simply say, 'Oh, it's their karma to suffer' and do nothing to help them. If the only use they make of their knowledge is to justify their own selfishness, it would sometimes be better for them if they had never heard of karma.

Westerners always want to do something to help when they hear that other people are suffering, and this is a truly superior quality. It is magnificent to see how, whenever there is a famine, an epidemic, floods or earthquakes, they immediately organize assistance.*

* Related reading: *The Seeds of Happiness,* Izvor No. 231, Chap. 12.

9 July

If you observe how nature purifies water, you will see that there are two possible methods. In the first method, water goes underground and discards its impurities as it seeps through the different layers of soil. In this way, it gradually becomes clear before re-emerging from a spring. In the second method, water is heated by the sun's rays; it becomes lighter and rises joyfully into the light of the earth's atmosphere in the form of vapour, and this process of evaporation is sufficient to purify it. Later, it falls back down to the ground in the form of dew or rain, bringing life to the vegetation on earth.

There are also two methods of purification for human beings. Those who refuse to be purified by the sun's rays are obliged to go underground, symbolically, and are subject to darkness and great pressure. But disciples choose the second method: they expose themselves to the light of the spiritual sun and purify themselves by rising to a higher level so as to absorb all the most luminous elements.*

* Related reading: *New Light on the Gospels,* Izvor No. 217, Chap. 10.

10 July

You have not yet given priority to the spiritual life. You are like children, always so fascinated by the people and events around you that you just stand and gape, oblivious to everything else. Your experience of the inner life has been too meagre to give you any idea of the extraordinary wealth this world contains. And not having experienced this, you have still not tasted the joys of the spirit. You say, 'Other people live better and possess much more than I do. What can I do with my poor spirituality? Look at all their wealth and success! If only I could be like them!'

But once you manage to taste sensations of a truly superior, divine order, no external veneer, no illusion will ever dazzle you or impede your spiritual growth again.

11 July

*H*ow do men and women look at each other? What do they see? They see the outward appearance, the body and the clothes, and this proves that they do not possess the true science. It is exactly as though, looking at a car, they saw only the chassis, and forgot all about the driver inside it, the one who thinks, feels and acts. But it is precisely this being whom you must accustom yourself to seek, to see and sense in others. Get into the habit of looking further, so as to discern their soul and spirit, for it is there that you will find wealth and great treasures – heaven itself.*

* Related reading: *The Seeds of Happiness,* Izvor No. 231, Chap. 19.

12 July

Suppose you are walking in the mountains and you amuse yourself by shouting a word out loud. What happens? The mountain sends the word back to you. The sound waves hit an obstacle and bounce back. It is exactly the same as when you throw a ball on the ground (it bounces upwards) or against a wall (it bounces back and hits you). This is a law of physics, and physical laws reflect spiritual laws. So, if you shout 'I love you!' the echo will come back to you from all sides: 'I love you... love you, love you.' And if you call out 'I hate you!' the echo will come back: 'I hate you... hate you, hate you.'

You must understand that exactly the same thing happens in life. By means of their thoughts, feelings and actions, humans constantly emit beneficial or harmful waves, and these waves travel through space until they encounter a wall, which sends the waves back to them. And what they receive is either a gift or a slap in the face. Yes, the boomerang effect!*

* Related reading: *Cosmic Moral Laws,* Complete Works, Vol. 12, Chap. 5.

13 July

New needs constantly arise in society, creating new problems and new activities. Life itself is responsible for this. Life flows and circulates, bringing with it new elements and turning in new directions, and humans are obliged to follow its lead. They have to go first one way and then another, or else they have to change the direction of the current, as is done for certain rivers.

Life refuses to let us stagnate; it forces us to explore all kinds of different places, in order to see, understand, feel and act in every possible way. So we must constantly search for solutions to the new problems life offers us. But, however diverse they may be, there are really three kinds of problems: they always concern either the intellect, the heart or the will, or if you prefer – but it comes to the same thing – the spirit, the soul or the physical body.*

* Related reading: *Golden Rules for Everyday Life,* Izvor No. 227, Chap. 55.

If someone who is telling you about an event or a scene that they have witnessed interposes their own point of view, feelings or impressions, you will not get a clear picture of what really happened. This is why you ask them to report only what they actually saw or heard: the people concerned, what they said or did, the objects, time and distances involved, exactly as though it had been filmed or recorded on tape. However, in asking them to confine themselves to the purely material, objective reality, you are asking them to speak of only one aspect of what happened, and this means that their report is necessarily incomplete. So in the end, you know no more about the exact reality than when the person was being subjective.

Human beings are more than an external form or a series of words and gestures; they possess an intangible inner life that emanates and spreads all round them, and if you neither see nor feel that life, and are incapable of describing or explaining it, you will miss a large part of the truth.*

* Related reading: *Truth, Fruit of Wisdom and Love,* Izvor No. 234, Chap. 11.

15 July

You must never abandon heaven for anyone – not even for a husband, wife or child – for it is only if you maintain contact with heaven that you can do them any good. If you turn your back on heaven in order to please others, you will lose everything, both heaven and earth. You will have neither the Lord nor those for whom you have made such great sacrifices; you will end up alone. If you seek heaven, on the other hand, you will also possess the earth, for the earth always follows, it submits itself to heaven and is at its service. Sooner or later, if you abandon heaven in order to cling to earth, the earth will slip from your grasp and you will be left with nothing.*

* Related reading: *Education Begins Before Birth,* Izvor No. 203, Chap. 5.

16 July

Someone says, 'I shall do exactly as I please!' Very well, do so. You will shove people aside, put your feet up on the table, eliminate whatever stands in your way, and behave in a thoroughly outrageous manner, but one day you will find yourself caught in a vice, for everything we do entails consequences. 'Caught?' you will say, 'Why should I be caught?' Because, whether you know it or not, by trying to assert your own power, you are constantly breaking the law, not only human law, but also – far more seriously – divine law as well. In this way, you are preparing the very worst conditions for your brain, your heart and your whole organism.

When human beings try to prove to themselves that they are strong and independent, they are taking a very dangerous path, for every time they break the law, they are adding another debt to those they already owe, and one day they will be crushed by the weight of those debts.

If you study the human digestive system, you will see that it is perfectly designed to receive and digest food, and discard anything that cannot be assimilated. If some element interferes with the proper working order of the kidneys or intestines, a person is gradually poisoned. This principle applies not only on the physical plane, but also on the etheric, astral and mental planes. If a person fails to eliminate the waste products of these planes, they will be poisoned by them too.*

A great many people already suffer from psychic poisoning because their astral and mental bodies are saturated with the waste produced by their chaotic thoughts and feelings. They do not realize that there are elements that must be expelled on those levels too. And how can they do this? By applying all the methods of purification proposed by Initiatic Science.**

* See note and figure on p. 394 and p. 395.

** Related reading: *Light is a Living Spirit,* Izvor No. 212, Chap. 7.

18 July

Water is alive and inhabited by very pure entities. This is why, before you make contact with water, whether in your bathroom or in nature, you should greet it with great love and respect, and ask the Angel of water to help you in your work.

It is not necessary to embark on all kinds of long and complicated ceremonies in order to purify yourself. Several times a day you have the opportunity to wash in water, and you should do so consciously, always remembering that the contact with physical water is simply a means of making contact with spiritual water, which is true water. Of course, washing oneself is one of the most ordinary things we do every day, but that is no reason to underestimate its importance. Like eating, sleeping and breathing, washing should be considered a sacred act that can liberate our soul.*

* Related reading: *The Mysteries of Fire and Water,* Izvor No. 232, Chap. 8.

Jesus said, *'My Father is still working and I am working with him.'* In saying this, he was calling on all humans to work for the establishment of the kingdom of God on earth. The question of exactly how long it will be before this comes about is not important. What is important – and this is something you must understand – is that as soon as you decide to participate in this gigantic, noble, divine work, and devote all your strength and energy to it, you are entering a new order of things; you are manifesting yourself as a true child of God.

It is very important to know for whom you are working and where your energies are being used. Without realizing it, those who participate in a dishonest enterprise become permeated with all the filth they stir up and end by destroying all the good they once possessed. You must participate in a grandiose, celestial enterprise. It does not matter whether it actually succeeds or not, or whether people understand and follow you or not; what matters is that you are doing some good work on yourself. Everything within you is improving, and it is you who benefit.*

* Related reading: *The True Meaning of Christ's Teaching,* Izvor No. 215, Chap. 4.

20 July

When the trunk and branches of a tree are all twisted, it shows that this particular tree has grown in the midst of great difficulties and that it has struggled to overcome those difficulties in order to survive. Its twisted trunk and branches reflect its struggles.

Similarly, we sometimes meet people whose features are crooked and deformed, but who are extremely gifted and talented. This shows that they too have had to overcome very difficult circumstances in order to develop. Unfortunately, they have often developed their intellectual faculties and willpower to the detriment of their moral qualities, and in doing so have deformed their faces. Beauty reflects a person's moral rather than their intellectual qualities. Those who are very beautiful are not always very intelligent. In fact, they are often ideal victims for those who are not so good looking but who have learned to exploit others. Beauty – true beauty – has more in common with kindness than with intelligence.*

* Related reading: *Creation: Artistic and Spiritual,* Izvor No. 223, Chap. 9.

21 July

When a truth dawns in the world, who is the first to sense it and receive it? The masses on the lower echelons, or the sages and Initiates who have reached a higher level? Which places on earth capture the first rays of the sun as it rises on the horizon? The plains and valleys or the mountaintops? Of course, you will all answer that it is the mountaintops, so how is it that you have never interpreted this phenomenon? Why is it that in life, everybody thinks that sages and Initiates are mistaken and that the majority, the masses, are right?

How could the Lord reveal himself to all sorts of people who have neither conscience nor morality, who stop at nothing to satisfy their lower nature and refuse his light, to those who live in the utmost purity and work tirelessly to reach him? This reasoning makes no sense. Is it the masses who are first to see the sun rising? No. Then why should you follow them? The first to be lit by the sun's rays, the first to show that they are attuned to light, the first to discover sublime truths, are the Initiates – genuine Initiates. It is they whom we should follow. As for those who remain on too low a level, God alone knows when the light will reach them!*

* Related reading: *Truth, Fruit of Wisdom and Love,* Izvor No. 234, Chap. 7.

22 July

Nothing in nature indicates that the spirit would like to rid itself of matter. On the contrary, we can see that it works on and through matter, and causes it to evolve. From the very beginning of the world, the spirit has shown that it wants to use matter and to transform and spiritualize it, to make it as vibrant as light. If the spirit refused to have anything more to do with matter, it would no longer be able to manifest itself, for it can manifest itself only through matter, which is its betrothed, its beloved wife.

Only ignorant human beings urge them to divorce. A Teaching that tells you to separate the spirit from matter should be left strictly alone. The one true philosophy tells us that the spirit has descended into matter in order to manifest itself through it. Of course, this is a gigantic task, but the spirit is never discouraged. It keeps coming back to celebrate its union with matter.*

* Related reading: *The Symbolic Language of Geometrical Figures,* Izvor No. 218, Chap. 3.

You are princes and princesses, and a kingdom awaits you. Why should you be discouraged and in despair simply because you have to wait a little longer for it? You complain, 'Yes, but in the meantime I'm living like a pauper; I wear myself out at work; nobody has any respect for me; people even insult me!' True, but in order to educate you, your father the king has sent you to do a short apprenticeship.

The Lord is wise and far-sighted. He says to himself, 'When this child begins to rule, he will have immense power over millions of creatures, but what will happen if he has never developed qualities of kindness, patience or courage? He will be mean, lazy, capricious and cowardly; he will behave like a tyrant and expect everyone to be at his service. This is why I will not let him come into his kingdom until he has shown proof that he will never abuse his power or his wealth.'*

* Related reading: *The Seeds of Happiness,* Izvor No. 231, Chap. 21.

24 July

*E*very idea is a highly intelligent living creature endowed with certain specific qualities. This is why, when you work for a divine idea, it acts upon you immediately, and gives you all its treasures. This idea, which dwells in the world of light, also introduces you to other regions and entities, and puts you in touch with all its friends.

It is written, *'Seek first the kingdom of God and his righteousness, and all these things will be given to you.'* Yes, because the idea of the kingdom of God becomes a bond between you and many other kindred ideas. Little by little, these ideas get to know you, and as each one owns a piece of land here or a house there, you gradually receive all these riches. Thanks to just one idea, all these blessings are yours. Yes, because on high everything is connected.*

* Related reading: *The High Ideal,* Brochure No. 307.

25 July

When you want to fulfil a desire of some kind, try never to neglect the moral aspect of it, otherwise you run the risk of committing serious mistakes. If you want to be rich, for instance, you must picture yourself sharing your wealth with those who are in need, and not be content to imagine how you will use it for your exclusive enjoyment. If you desire beauty, here too you have to be careful: do not seek the kind of beauty that wreaks havoc in human hearts, and drives them to despair or to crime. Concentrate on spiritual beauty, the beauty that inspires and elevates others, and propels them towards heaven.

The tragedy of human beings is that they never bring moral consideration to bear on their plans and projects. Even when they join a spiritual teaching, many people do so only in the hope of finding ways of gratifying their personal desires.*

* Related reading: *Man's Psychic Life: Elements and Structures,* Izvor No. 222, Chap. 5.

Jesus said, *'Love your enemies'* but this is very difficult to do. There are not many people, even among Christians, who have made up their minds to love their enemies. We do not even know how to love our friends properly, so how can we possibly love our enemies? Analyze yourselves and you will see that this is the most difficult thing in the world, and yet there is one being who has fulfilled this commandment perfectly, and that is the sun. Whatever you do, the sun will continue to send you its light and warmth. The sun is the only one that has ever solved the problem; it even loves, nourishes and vivifies unbelievers and criminals.

If you want to understand the highest moral law, you will find it in the sun, nowhere else. Other people talk, but they never practise what they preach; whereas the sun does not preach, it only practises. It will never say, 'I love you all; I love my enemies!' No, the sun does not say a word, but it continues to give them light and warmth.

27 July

Many people think that they are strong enough to do whatever they like with impunity. No; if they do wrong, sooner or later they will suffer from the disorder* created within them by their bad actions, for their conscience will be troubled, and they will lose their inner peace. Even a magus, who commands the whole of nature and who is obeyed by the spirits, is not exempt from this law, because there is no power in existence capable of restoring the peace of someone who is tormented by the consciousness of guilt.

You must rely neither on your strength nor on your will, but only on your good, honourable actions. This is the only way to be free. As soon as you break a law, you lose all your powers, and they will be restored to you only when you make amends for your misdeeds. The difference between true magi and ordinary human beings is that magi always correct their mistakes very quickly. This is where their power lies, in their ability to make amends. As long as they have not corrected their errors, they are powerless to ease their conscience. But as soon as reparation is made, this acts indirectly on their conscience, and their peace is restored.

* Related reading: *Man's Subtle Bodies and Centres,* Izvor No. 219, Chap. 3.

28 July

When we concentrate on the sun, which is the centre of our universe, we draw closer to our own centre, our higher Self, our inner sun; we unite with it and begin, little by little, to resemble it.

But to concentrate on the sun also means to mobilize all one's thoughts, feelings and desires in the service of the highest possible ideal. Those who work to unify the multitude of conflicting forces that try to pull them every which way, and launch them in a single, luminous, salutary direction, become such a potent focal point that they are able to radiate light throughout space. Yes, human beings who succeed in mastering the leanings of their lower nature become like the sun and impart something beneficial to the whole of humankind. Their freedom is such that their field of consciousness expands to the dimensions of the whole human race, on whom they pour out the superabundance of light and love that flows from their own being.*

* Related reading: *Toward a Solar Civilization,* Izvor No. 201.

Do not worry about whether or not others appreciate your good qualities. The only thing that matters is your own work. The laws are absolutely faithful and true, and one day, if you do your work honestly, everybody will be forced to recognize you for what you are.

Imagine a gardener who has just planted a very special, extraordinary seed. If he is so stupid that every time he has a visitor, he digs it up and shows it to them saying, 'See this seed? Well, I planted it. Take a look – it will grow into a wonderful tree and produce delicious fruit. We'll soon be able to eat some.', even if he runs and puts it back in the earth at once, that will be the end of the poor tree! Well, this is exactly what many people tend to do. They dig up a seed that they have just planted because they want other people to know what a magnificent tree they are growing. But in doing this, they kill it! You should not dig up your seeds; you must wait until the tree appears for all to see.*

* Related reading: *On the Art of Teaching (Part III)*, Complete Works, Vol. 29, Chap. 5.

Those who do not participate in the collective life do not realize to what extent they are limiting themselves. They move within the narrow circle of their own desires, appetites and feelings, and never think of others. How paltry and pathetic! This limited state is normal for a child, but not for an adult. An adult must show that they are able to think of others: of wife or husband, children, but also of colleagues or employees, and so on. And even this is very limited. Their circle must expand more and more to encompass their country, race, and the whole of humankind – and even further, until it embraces immensity, infinity.

Rare are those who break free and reach beyond all limitations, those whose desires, thoughts and interests all converge on the collectivity, the universal dimension of life; but it is towards this that we must endeavour to work. *

* Related reading: *A New Dawn: Society and Politics in the Light of Initiatic Science (Part I),* Complete Works, Vol. 25, Chap. 2.

31 July

*H*uman beings are accustomed to nourishing themselves on solid, liquid and gaseous elements, and that is all. But what do they do with the fourth element, the igneous element, fire, light? Not much. They do not know how to nourish themselves with light, and yet light is even more vital than air.*

Humans need to nourish themselves with light for the sake of their brain, for the brain also needs to eat, and light is the food of the brain. It is light that awakens the faculties that give us access to the divine world. You will say that when you eat and drink and breathe, you are nourishing your whole body, and that includes your brain. That is true, but as long as you are content to nourish your brain only with solid, liquid and gaseous particles, which are not the elements it most needs, your powers of understanding will continue to be very limited. Tradition tells us that Zarathustra once asked the god Ahura Mazda what the first man ate, and Ahura Mazda replied, 'He ate fire, and drank light.'

* Related reading: *Hrani Yoga – The Alchemical and Magical Meaning of Nutrition,* Complete Works, Vol. 16, Chap. 1.

1 August

Suppose someone thinks to himself, 'I will never bow to others. No one is going to step on my toes and anyone who gets in my way had better look out!' Well, it is impossible for such a decision not to have an effect on their character as well as on their behaviour and their relations with others. They will become increasingly suspicious, arrogant, harsh and vindictive, and everything they do will have the same aim: power, domination and violence. This is how, with one thing leading to another, they will be in danger of drifting into crime and you all know how that story ends!

Similarly, those whose goal is money, pleasure or renown also embark on a set course, and they too will be unable to avoid the consequences of their choice. So, be very careful about the decisions* and plans you make for the future; try to foresee what they might lead to.

* Related reading: *Man, Master of his Destiny,* Izvor No. 202, Chap. 5.

2 August

You all have a tendency to wish for ease, success and prosperity in preference to all the rest, and this is natural. Yes, until you are forced to admit that lucidity, fortitude, patience, purity and kindness are acquisitions that are far more precious. For once you possess these qualities, you are armed against all the difficulties everyone inevitably encounters in life; whereas without them, your most brilliant successes may well turn to disaster.

Indeed, you must not believe that apparently favourable conditions and effortless success are necessarily what is best; they are often pitfalls for those who have not developed certain moral qualities.* Open your eyes to what goes on around you and you will no longer wish for certain kinds of easy success nor envy those who have them.

* Related reading: *Man, Master of his Destiny*, Izvor No. 202, Chap. 6.

3 August

It is pointless to decide to limit the physical manifestations of love unless it is to savour its spiritual manifestations more fully. Besides, someone who renounces physical love without seeking love on the spiritual plane* is running a great risk, for restraint can very quickly become repression.

This means that continence and chastity must not be thought of as a deprivation. You must not deprive yourself; you must simply move to a different level, that is to say, you must do what you have always done but on a higher plane. Instead of drinking from a swamp full of microbes, drink from a crystal-clear spring. If you stop drinking altogether you will die. If you have been told that you must not drink, it is because you must not drink water from a sewer. You must drink – but you must drink heavenly water.

* Related reading: *Sexual Force or the Winged Dragon*, Izvor No. 205, Chap. 8.

4 August

When human beings dig in their heels and refuse to understand, the only way they can be taught anything is through suffering. This is not a very desirable solution, but what other way is there? When Cosmic Intelligence, which is wise and all-loving, has tried every means; when it has tried wisdom and explanations by way of the Initiates it has sent; when it has tried love and patience by sending saints, prophets and martyrs, and there is still no change, the only hope that remains of educating human beings is to send them hardship. Cosmic Intelligence never begins by using suffering. Only when it has tried everything else does it have recourse to suffering in order to make human beings think.*

* Related reading: *Man, Master of his Destiny,* Izvor No. 202, Chap. 8.

5 August

Some people ask, 'Why should we pray to God?' The truth is that God does not need our prayers, but He has equipped us with certain devices and tells us, 'Switch them on yourselves for they are well built and they will work!' You have all seen those automatic vending machines in stations that dispense food and drinks. It is you who make them work; the station attendant does not need to get involved. In the same way, God does not need to get involved in the functioning of our inner machines. It is enough that he has given them to us, and it is our job to put the coins in the slot and make them work. If you pray correctly, you will get results because your prayer is the coin you put in the slot.

Every time you pray, you release a force both inside and outside yourself and this force sets certain wheels in motion. This is why you feel peace, joy and beauty flooding into you. The effects are both internal and external.

6 August

*H*ere on earth, our spirit cannot manifest itself fully because it is bound by the limitations of matter. In its own realm, in the world above, it has unlimited possibilities, it is all-powerful. Only when it is imprisoned in matter is it limited. But thanks to our ongoing, daily efforts, the spirit gradually breaks through and in the end, it manages to transform and overcome every obstacle.

The spirit is said to possess 'supernatural' powers. No, there is nothing supernatural about it.* Miracles and wonders – all those events that seem to run counter to the laws of nature – are neither supernatural, nor unnatural. They simply conform to other laws that are equally natural: the laws of the spirit.

* Related reading: *Freedom, the Spirit Triumphant,* Izvor No. 211, Chap. 3.

7 *August*

A woman knows instinctively that it is to her advantage to be beautiful, so she takes care of her figure, her hair and her complexion and she puts on make-up, which of course produces immediate results. Men notice her and she has the satisfaction of feeling that she is pretty and attractive.

Yes, but what kind of people will she attract in this way? Certainly not Initiates! Only idiots, sensual men or louts, who ask nothing more of a woman than to be delectable so that they can well and truly devour her! On the other hand, if a woman works to acquire inner beauty* by developing her qualities and virtues, she will attract quite a different class of men, men who are intelligent, honest and generous, and who will help and protect her and give her every opportunity to fulfil herself.

* Related reading: *Creation: Artistic and Spiritual,* Izvor No. 223, Chap. 9.

8 August

*T*hose whose field of vision is too narrow cannot be happy. That is why egotists cannot be happy; everything about them has shrunk. If you want to be happy, you must stretch yourself until you are wide open and able to embrace the whole world, and only love makes this possible. Those who are full of love stretch and expand. They embrace and vibrate in harmony with the whole universe, and everything in the universe opens up to them. They know no barriers and happiness never abandons them.

The pre-condition for happiness* is love; not science, not philosophy, only love. Science and knowledge cannot bring you happiness; they can only pave the way, guide you and give you some light, but they are incapable of making you happy. Solomon understood this. He said, *'For in much wisdom is much grief, and he who increases knowledge increases sorrow.'* Those who know a great deal are not happy; those whose hearts are full of love, even if they do not know much, are far happier.

---

* Related reading: *The Seeds of Happiness,* Izvor No. 231, Chap. 1.

9 August

Life is a faithful reflection of yourself. If you say that life is beautiful it is because you are beautiful.* And if you think that it is absurd or hideous, is it not because you are catching a glimpse of yourself in a mirror?

Life is in our image: we see in it only what we have within us. This is why each life is different from every other. We speak about 'life' thinking that we know what we are talking about. We imagine that everybody has the same degree and the same quality of life, but this is not so. Each individual speaks of 'life' only on their own level and from their own experience of it. But we do not know what true life is, in all its breadth and splendour and immensity. The most we can do is get a little closer to it, and we can only do this if we are able to restore the ties that link us to the world of the soul and the spirit.

* Related reading: *'In Spirit and in Truth'*, Izvor No. 235, Chap. 3.

10 August

When you come up against difficulties in your life, you must neither rebel against them nor try to avoid them. Try to understand that if Cosmic Intelligence has put you in this situation it is in order to push you to go a step further, a step higher. Do not wish for everything to be smooth in life.

Mountaineers would never get to the top of a mountain if the face were perfectly smooth. In order to pull themselves up, they need the rough edges that give them a foothold or a handhold, and something to which they can attach their rope. In this way, little by little, they climb up to the top. Well, we need the difficulties, sorrows and obstacles that life brings because they serve exactly the same purpose.

11 August

Perhaps, one day, walking through the countryside you have seen a little girl keeping watch over cows in a field. Beside her sits a loving dog that helps her to herd the cows. Suddenly one of the animals strays into the neighbour's field and the girl sends her dog to bring it back. The faithful dog runs off barking and nipping at the cow's heels until it is safely back in its master's field. Afterwards, the dog comes back and lies beside the little girl again, satisfied that it has done a good job and ready to obey her again.

This explains the role set out for the devil.* As long as human beings are careful not to break any laws or wander off into forbidden territory, they will not be tormented or pursued. But as soon as they stray, the Creator sends the devil to chivvy them and nip at their heels, that is to say, to give them all kinds of problems. The devil may seem like a fierce dog that is hostile to human beings, but as soon as they begin to behave themselves, he leaves them alone.

* Related reading: *Man, Master of his Destiny,* Izvor No. 202, Chap. 2.

12 August

Learn to work with divine love,* to kindle it within you and shed its light on all living creatures, on all things, even trees, mountains and oceans. In this way, your existence will bring good to the whole world. Even when you are alone, you can speak words of peace, hope and joy for all men and women on earth, knowing that your words will have an effect.

Always try to improve the situation around you by thoughts and words that add something positive. Begin by trying to create harmony and light in yourself (for you cannot give others something you do not possess), and then when you sense that harmony and light are a reality within you, project them outwards. This is what it means to work with divine love.

* Related reading: *Man, Master of his Destiny,* Izvor No. 202, Chap. 4.

13 August

It sometimes happens that you walk down a street and pass a place where criminals are doing something dishonest. If at that moment your own inner state is negative, your vibrations will be tuned to those produced by the crimes that are going on nearby, and you will be influenced by them. You may even be driven to do something wrong yourself without realizing that it is because of the fluidic emanations you picked up as you walked by. This is why it is so important to pay attention to the quality of your inner disposition; it is the only effective way of defending yourself against negative influences.

It is no good relying on charms, talismans or any of the trinkets that charlatans sell on almost every street corner nowadays.* You yourself must work on your own thoughts and feelings so as to attract only the purest and most luminous currents.

* Related reading: *Looking into the Invisible,* Izvor No. 228, Chap. 5.

14 August

A human being's inner face is different from their physical face. Our inner face is the face of our soul,* and it has no clearly and unalterably defined features by which it can be recognized. It is so closely dependent on our psychic life, on our thoughts and feelings that it is constantly changing – it will be luminous or sombre, harmonious or twisted, expressive or wooden, depending on the moment. This is the face we have to model, sculpt, paint and illuminate through prayer, meditation, contemplation and an elevated state of consciousness, so that one day it will imbue our physical face.

* Related reading: *Man's Subtle Bodies and Centres,* Izvor No. 219, Chap. 1.

15 August

Mountain peaks are inhabited by very luminous and powerful entities that are attracted to their exceptional atmosphere of purity. The reason why we should go up into the mountains is to get in touch with these entities. But this requires a great deal of knowledge, and that knowledge is open only to those who have committed themselves heart and soul to the path of light.*

Very few people know how to take advantage of the favourable conditions offered by mountains for their spiritual evolution. They go to the mountains to have fun and make a lot of noise. They have no respect for the entities that inhabit these regions. This is why mountains, which are both sensitive and intelligent, remain closed to them. There may even come a time when these entities will abandon their mountain dwellings because they are so disturbed by the humans who sully everything. You at least must try to have an attitude that shows them how much you appreciate their presence and the work they do.

* Related reading: *The Mysteries of Fire and Water,* Izvor No. 232, Chap. 7.

16 August

*T*he young people of today think that in obtaining sexual freedom they have won a great victory. That is true: it is a great victory over the hypocrisy and narrow-mindedness that prevailed for centuries. But has this really solved the problem of sexuality? After repression comes release... and now the door is open to every kind of physical and psychic disorder. It is no good thinking that the problems will be solved by teaching people to use condoms and contraceptives or by legalizing abortion; and to forbid these things is just as pointless. It is not a question either of permitting or forbidding anything, but of studying and trying to understand.

Sexual energy* is an age-old force against which it is useless to struggle. That does not mean that we have to be enslaved by it; we have to know that there are ways of channelling and directing it to further our psychic, moral and spiritual growth. It is up to each individual, once they have sought and received these explanations, to reflect and decide how they want to behave.

* Related reading: *Sexual Force or the Winged Dragon*, Izvor No. 205, Chap. 3.

17 August

    Choral singing in four parts corresponds on the physical plane to an exercise we should do every day, several times a day, to bring our heart, mind, soul and spirit into harmony. Four-part singing is also, of course, a symbol of the effort we should make to attune ourselves and harmonize with each other. The blending of voices above our heads is, at the same time, a blending of our subtle bodies.

    The four voices – bass, tenor, alto and soprano – also correspond to the four strings of a violin, which is a symbol of man. The G string represents the heart; the D represents the mind; the A represents the soul, and the E represents the spirit. The body of the violin represents the human body and the bow represents the will, which acts upon the four principles of heart, mind, soul and spirit.

18 August

Matter is so diverse and rich that there will always be things to see, hear, touch, taste and acquire. This is why human beings, who first began to explore matter many thousands of years ago, sometimes forget themselves and become lost in it; our modern age is an increasingly giddy descent of human consciousness ever deeper into matter.

But even if matter is inexhaustible, it can satisfy our needs only on the physical plane.* Eventually, there will come a time when human beings begin to feel satiated, saturated, and they will feel the need to climb back to the regions of the spirit. They will sense that by returning to the heights, they will retrieve all the riches they had to leave behind when they descended into matter. Not only will they regain these riches, but they will also have a far better understanding of things, and will be able to benefit fully from all that they have acquired on the physical plane, where there is so much to study, work at and enjoy.

* Related reading: *The True Meaning of Christ's Teaching*, Izvor No. 215, Chap. 5.

19 August

Because I speak to you only about realities that exist within you – even if you are not yet aware of them and do not understand them – I know that my words touch something in you that yearns to be brought out into the light. It is like a lotus that begins by growing underwater before opening its petals on the surface.

Things are born, take form and begin to grow in the darkness of the subconscious. When they finally appear on the level of consciousness, they are not at their first beginnings, but nearly at their completion, for they have been in motion for a long time. In the same way, my words awaken something in the deepest part of your being that will one day rise like a lotus* and blossom above the water.

* Related reading: *The Seeds of Happiness,* Izvor No. 231, Chap. 19.

20 August

You know the parable of the prodigal son* who left his father's house to go in search of adventure in the world and who, having encountered only trials and disappointment, returned at last to his father's house. All the sacred books contain images and stories that illustrate this twofold process: departure and return, involution and evolution.

And when alchemists speak of the two operations, 'solve' and 'coagula', they are presenting the same process in another way. Nature itself speaks to us of this. You can look up and see clear blue skies and a moment later it is as though a veil were drawn across the sky. The water vapour in the atmosphere condenses and forms clouds, and in a little while the clouds disappear and the sky is blue again. Everywhere throughout the universe you can see this phenomenon of alternation between appearance and disappearance, birth and death, creation and the return to nothingness. It is a message from nature, an invitation to disciples to reflect and understand.

* Related reading: *Freedom, the Spirit Triumphant,* Izvor No. 211, Chap. 8.

21 August

'To know, to will, to dare, to keep silent.'* This fourfold axiom sums up the science of Initiates. Why 'keep silent'? you ask. Because if you know what you have to do, if you have the will to do it and dare to begin the work, there is nothing more to say. The results of your work will be expressed in your whole being. When you dwell in peace and joy, is it necessary to tell others about it? No, they can see and feel it. And if a storm is raging within you, it is no good telling people that you are floating in a state of serenity and harmony – they will not believe you. They will only laugh in your face because here too, everything – all your internal disorder and tumult – shows through.

Human beings talk and talk; they try to convince others by their eloquence, but reality speaks for itself. The trouble is that people's words say one thing while reality often says something quite different. This is why the precept 'keep silent' is something you need to meditate on.

* Related reading: *The Book of Divine Magic,* Izvor No. 226, Chap. 1.

22 *August*

When you are distressed,* it is as though you had been injected with a toxic substance, and you must not just accept it and do nothing about it. Instead of waiting passively for the torment to disappear, you must work either to get rid of it or to transform it. A true magus is someone who has learned to treat every event that happens to him as raw material that he must craft. This is what makes him strong and powerful, whereas those who submit passively, without reacting, will face a lifetime of defeat.

Our instincts and selfish impulses also represent raw material, and we must not just leave them in their primitive state; we must add a spiritual element to them. As matter is nothing but a condensation of energy, it is up to human beings to transform that energy. In doing so they enter the realm of alchemy and magic.

* Related reading: *True Alchemy or the Quest for Perfection,* Izvor No. 221, Chap. 1.

23 *August*

You must never accept inertia. Even the sick and disabled must try to make some small gesture, take one small step. And if a person truly cannot make the slightest physical movement, they can still use their mental powers to imagine that they are moving about and doing exactly the things they used to do. This mental activity breaks the ground, opens up a furrow, and so creates the right conditions for physical activity to be restored.

24 August

The consciousness of an Initiate* lives in other people; this is why he can nourish them with his light from a distance. Physical food can nourish only those who eat it, and while it is true that a woman nourishes the child in her womb for a time, as soon as the child is born, it leads a separate life and has to eat for itself.

On the spiritual plane, a Master has to nourish his disciples, at least to begin with. He 'eats' light and in eating it he nourishes his disciples. Just as a mother carries a child in her womb, a Master takes his children into his soul and consciousness to nourish them until they are capable of nourishing themselves. From then on, they will in turn be able to nourish others. Disciples are bound to their Master just as a foetus is bound to its mother; when the Master receives strength from heaven, his disciples also benefit.

* Related reading: *What is a Spiritual Master?*, Izvor No. 207, Chap. 6.

25 August

Initiates teach that instead of spending our lives trying to acquire external powers, which will never really belong to us, it is far better to work to acquire those powers inwardly. This is the task before us, this is what we must work at, for true strength lies within;* it dwells in a living, thinking, active being, capable of decision and constructive organization.

This is why the Initiates have given us rules and methods that allow the complete, perfect and absolute manifestation of that being who contains all things and disposes of all things: the spirit. You are familiar with the formula given by Master Peter Deunov: 'Niama sila kato silata na douha; samo silata na douha e sila bojia.' 'There is no strength like the strength of the spirit; only the strength of the spirit is the strength of God.' It is in the spirit that we must look for strength, for true strength is in the will and intelligence of the spirit.

* Related reading: *The Powers of Thought,* Izvor No. 224, Chap. 5.

*T*he problem of evil cannot be resolved by reason, for it is beyond human understanding. In reality evil does not exist; it exists only for those who are weak and unprepared, who do not know how to use it. But for the children of God, for Initiates and spiritual Masters, evil – this infernal element that religious believers talk about so much and understand so little – is a rich and precious substance that can be exploited and used for the realization of fantastic things.* Initiates, because they are very strong and pure, have the courage to confront evil by plunging into the depths of their own nature, and their courage enables them to bring back many valuable pearls. They are like pearl-fishers who dive to the bottom of the ocean and bring pearl oysters back to the surface without being devoured by sharks or ensnared by seaweed.

But experiences of this kind are not for everyone. There are very few people on earth who are capable of descending into the depths of their own nature so as to illuminate and sublimate what they find there and transform it into something beautiful.

* Related reading: *The Tree of the Knowledge of Good and Evil,* Izvor No. 210, Chap. 2.

27 August

You are all under the protection of the entities of the sun because one day I dedicated the Brotherhood to the sun.* Why did I do this? In order to open a door for the luminous entities of the sun so that these powerful, highly evolved spirits can enter and work on you from within. This consecration does not apply only to those who were present at the time; it applies to all those who, in the future, will come to know our Teaching, the Teaching of the sun. Now that you are consecrated, solar spirits can enter you and work through you, for this is the purpose of a consecration whether of an object, a place, or a person: it creates an opening for the spirits to which it is dedicated.

This is why the spirits of the sun can now help and heal you and give you revelations.

* Related reading: *Toward a Solar Civilization,* Izvor No. 201, Chap. 4.

28 August

You want to be free and independent, but at the same time, you always want others to think of you and help you, and even to act and work in your place. Well, it is time you understood that if you really want to be free, you must learn not to count too much on the help of others. Other people have their own worries and problems, and they will think of you one day and forget you the next.

And even if everybody were always ready to help you, you would still feel that something was missing. Why? Because you cannot get what you truly need from someone else, you must work to get it for yourself. What you need most is to become more sensible, stronger, more patient and enlightened – in other words, freer. Only you can achieve this through your own efforts.*

* Related reading: *Freedom, the Spirit Triumphant,* Izvor No. 211.

29 August

*T*he skin is a reflection of our inner being: you can tell a great deal about someone simply by looking at their skin, for something in the texture and colour speaks immediately of a spiritual life or an ordinary, coarse life.

It is also interesting to note that a person's skin is different in different parts of their body: in some places, it is smooth and finely textured while in others it is discoloured or wrinkled. There are even people whose skin, although white, appears to have a mauve, blue or yellow tint. This shows that behind the visible façade of the skin, there are other skins that we cannot see and which project pure or impure particles. Indeed, the skin is a language that we should learn to read and interpret.

To find the meaning of life is to find an element that only the divine world can give;* and it gives it only to those who persevere for years and years in their efforts to reach it. For the meaning of life is the reward given for the patient, unceasing inner work of transformation that a person has undertaken on themselves.

Once a person reaches a certain level of consciousness, they receive an electron from heaven, which like a drop of light, permeates the matter of their whole being. From then on, their life takes on a new dimension, a new intensity, and they see events with new clarity, as though they had been given to understand the meaning of everything. Even death is no longer feared, because this electron reveals to them the immensity of the eternal world in which there are no more dangers, no more darkness. They sense that they are already walking in the limitless world of light.

* Related reading: *Life Force,* Complete Works, Vol. 5, Chap. 8.

31 August

It is human beings' lower nature that urges them to neglect their work and responsibilities and to do only what gives them pleasure. But those who always try to avoid every effort or difficulty must know that they will inevitably encounter even greater problems. Instead of sidestepping their problems, they would do better to look for solutions; otherwise they will find themselves in situations far worse than those they tried to avoid.

Until we have solved a problem and learned what the invisible world intends us to learn from it, there is nowhere we can run to for escape. Wherever we go, we will only find ourselves faced with even harder lessons. The invisible world says, 'You refused to learn anything there, so now you have something else to learn here!' We must not run away from difficulties,* but endeavour to understand what they mean, and do whatever is necessary to resolve them. Once we have managed to do so, everything else we undertake from then on will be beneficial.

* Related reading: *Golden Rules for Everyday Life,* Izvor No. 227, Chap. 44 and 45.

1 September

If there were laboratories equipped with sufficiently sophisticated instruments, it could be proved that some humans exude fluidic emanations so strong that they can asphyxiate small animals. It could also be shown that the opposite is true, that emanations from a spiritual being are beneficial to all creatures. The presence of such a selfless, loving being has a favourable effect on all those around them. Even spirits who have already left this earth come to them to be nourished by their emanations, for they have overcome human weaknesses. Such a being is concerned only with spreading peace and light all around them.* It is thanks to beings such as these that the atmosphere on earth has not yet become completely unbreathable.

---

* Related reading: *The Powers of Thought*, Izvor No. 224, Chap. 3.

2 September

When a child is born into a family, do its parents know where it came from, what its background is, and why it was born to them in particular? It often happens that children are born into a certain family because, in a past life, they had some form of relationship with their present parents. A boy may have been engaged, married or in love with the woman who is now his mother, and the same is true of a girl and her father. Having once known love between them in one form, they must now, in the course of their evolution, experience it in another form.

Ordinary physical love has to evolve. If today a man and a woman feel a sexual attraction for each other, in their next incarnation they may well be parent and child. They will kiss each other again, but their embrace will be that of parent and child, which is more evolved, more spiritual in nature.*

* Related reading: *Man, Master of his Destiny,* Izvor No. 202, Chap. 8.

3 September

To know something or someone means to enter into their heart, and the only way to do this is to identify with them,* that is to say, to meld with them. If only for a moment, you have to become the person or thing you want to know, and this is not possible if you are content to look at them from the outside. You have to get inside them and sense every vibration of their being. The intellect cannot do this. This is something that only the spirit can do.

Now, for the practical application of this: if you strive every day with your spirit and your love to identify with the Supreme Being, the Source of life, the First Cause, the Father of all creation, one day you will begin to feel that God is living within you, with all His glory, power, wisdom and love.

* Related reading: *Man's Two Natures: Human and Divine,* Izvor No. 213, Chap. 3.

4 September

Only those who love others should be allowed to prepare their food, so that it may be filled exclusively with harmonious vibrations. You will say, 'But if the food is fresh and wholesome, and contains no toxic substances, surely that is enough?' Of course, it is wholly desirable that food should not be polluted, but it is also important that those preparing it realize that the food that passes through their hands receives their spiritual emanations, which it then transmits to those who eat it.

Food is prepared by hand, and our hands are the magic agents through which something of our own quintessence is transmitted. Cooks, bakers, pastry chefs and all those who cook every day for their family should know of this magical chemical law. Then they will handle food in the conscious knowledge that it is going to help build the bodies of people near or far, known or unknown. This is a huge responsibility, and it is important to be in the best possible state when preparing food, keeping in your mind thoughts of peace, light and good health for those who will eat it.*

* Related reading: *Golden Rules for Everyday Life,* Izvor No. 227, Chap. 109.

5 September

Love is implacable toward hatred; light is implacable toward darkness; good is implacable toward evil. If you swallow poison, it will do you immeasurable harm, but a powerful antidote will soon set you right. Of course, the effects of the antidote seem less spectacular than those of the poison, but they are just as powerful.

Good is as powerful and as amazing as evil, but as it suits us, we think that it is only normal, and pay little or no attention to it. But if you ask evil its opinion of good, it will say, 'Oh dear, don't talk to me about good! The knocks I have received from it!' Ask the spirits of darkness what effect a spirit of light has on them and they will scream and flee in terror. We cannot see all this so we never think about it, but if you want to understand the power of good,* you need to question evil about it.

* Related reading: *Love Greater Than Faith,* Izvor No. 239, Chap. 7.

6 September

*T*he secret of white magic is the right attitude;* if you have the right attitude you have the
magic word that will enable you to communicate
not only with humans, but also with animals,
plants, stones or inanimate objects. Each of you
must find this attitude on your own, for yourself.

The only rule I can give you is that in order to
find this attitude, you must cultivate within you a
genuine respect for all that exists. Stop thinking
that when you behave in an uncaring and
disrespectful manner, you are proving yourself
to be strong and independent. No, this failing,
now so common among our contemporaries, is
the root of all misfortunes.

* Related reading: *The Tree of the Knowledge of Good and
Evil,* Izvor No. 210, Chap. 2.

7 September

*P*arents must try to understand the subtle relationship that very young children have with the visible and invisible worlds, for children possess a sensitivity that adults have lost. This sensitivity stems from our distant past, when humans were aware of being at one with the living organism of nature.* This is why children perceive animals, plants, stones and objects as living beings to whom they can talk and with whom they are friends.

Some children are even in touch with nature spirits; they see them, smile at them, and have long conversations with them, listening to them and replying. But little by little, this contact is lost because of the attitudes of adults, the things they say and the way they bring up their children. For the good of their children, but also for their own inner development, parents should give this question some thought. They should observe their children throughout their early years, so as to read the true secrets of life in the book of their children's soul.

* Related reading: *The Wellsprings of Eternal Joy,* Izvor No. 242, Chap. 16.

8 September

God wanted human beings to be free* to choose their own destiny, and the spirits from above have no right to intervene in this choice. If humans decide to get themselves in trouble, the spirits must let them do so. The proof of this is that over the last several million years, the spirits have never interfered when humans fought amongst themselves and inflicted great suffering on each other. They wait patiently, knowing that sooner or later even the most stubborn of humans will eventually understand – they have the whole of eternity in which to do so! If a person wishes to become a saint, they let them do so. If someone decides to be a criminal, they again let him do as he chooses. But these spirits know that there are laws governing all of these things, and that the criminal will suffer and come to grief. They can foresee this but they leave everyone learn for themselves, and draw their own conclusions. We are free therefore to do as we please. The laws will punish us for our evil deeds and reward us for our good deeds, but the choice of doing good or evil is left to us.

* Related reading: *Truth, Fruit of Wisdom and Love,* Izvor No. 234, Chap. 18.

9 September

*E*verything that human beings think, feel or want flows into the invisible world and sets in motion forces and powers, whether of good or evil. But as most people do not know this, there are billions of individuals on earth who unwittingly spend their days triggering destructive forces. If you try to enlighten them, they look at you with astonishment, wondering what on earth you are talking about, for as everyone knows, thoughts and feelings can be neither seen nor touched, so how can they possibly trigger events?

The inner life,* the life of thought, is vital for the construction not only of our own future but also of that of all humankind. This is why the first thing that we learn in an initiatic school is how to monitor our thoughts, feelings and desires, and to see the direction they are taking, and where they will lead, in order to link up with the beneficial forces of nature and work towards our own development and that of the whole world.

* Related reading: *True Alchemy or the Quest for Perfection,* Izvor No. 221, Chap. 4.

10 September

*M*oney is useful only on a material level. On the psychic or spiritual plane it can serve no good purpose. On these planes what is needed is light, the light that is liquid gold.* If you love the light, then you already possess gold on the spiritual plane. The more you have of this type of gold, the more you can 'buy' in the celestial shops – things unobtainable elsewhere, such as wisdom, love, joy, infinity and eternity.

This is why the sages and the Initiates try to amass as much gold as possible on the spiritual plane, in order to enrich themselves with qualities and virtues that they can then use for the good of others. Even if they have no money in their pockets, thanks to their light, they can still draw down blessings from heaven on all around them.

* Related reading: *The Seeds of Happiness,* Izvor No. 231, Chap. 5.

11 September

It can happen that people, who have for years been absolute pillars of morality and virtue, suddenly fall prey to an all-consuming passion, and start to indulge in all kinds of excesses and vice. Conversely, we have heard of people who have committed crimes or lived a life of debauchery, who then become saints and models of goodness, purity and sacrifice. Both scenarios are difficult to comprehend, and yet they become intelligible if we know that for human beings, as for trees, the highest is linked to the lowest, and vice-versa.

Have you noticed how the branches of trees are linked to the roots? As the branches grow, becoming longer and thicker, the roots also develop, sinking deeper and deeper into the ground. So long as human beings do not know how the higher world is linked with the lower world,* and do not look to Initiatic Science to find out how this link works, many phenomena of their psychic life will remain impossible for them to control.

* Related reading: *Man's Two Natures: Human and Divine,* Izvor No. 213, Chap. 2.

12 September

*A*n Initiate says, 'I will deprive myself of these few grains of wheat so that I can then harvest thousands'. And instead of eating these grains, he sows them and ends up harvesting a whole field. Whereas an ordinary person says, 'Why should I go without? I will eat all these grains.' Yes, but after a while they have nothing left. We have to learn to ration ourselves and go without a few grains in order to sow them and reap an abundant harvest in the future. We must eat, but just enough; the rest should be sown.

Obviously, these grains of wheat are symbolic. We should be learning to sow the seeds of our thoughts and feelings, which can work for the good of all on condition that we do not eat them, in other words that we do not use them for our own selfish pursuits. Those who know how to ration themselves will reap such an abundant harvest that they will be able to feed the whole world.*

* Related reading: *The Wellsprings of Eternal Joy,* Izvor No. 242, Chap. 7.

13 September

*A*dvances in technology are providing more and more devices and products to repair, patch up and clean all the mistakes and blunders made by humans – and what publicity there is for all these products! But no one seems interested in the psychological and moral aspects of the question, that is, how to make humans more conscious of their thoughts and gestures. Why be careful, why pay attention when there are pharmacies, hospitals, garages and laundry services?

Extraordinary progress has been made in the external field, but in the inner areas of life, it is deplorable. And then we talk about the economy! True economy* is to be careful and sensible. The other economy, that of financial economists, is really nothing but spending and ruin. If you want to practise real economy and enrich yourself with treasures that you can use to help others, you must be more careful, enlightened, in control of yourself and sensible. It is as simple as that.

* Related reading: *Under the Dove, the Reign of Peace,* Izvor No. 208, Chap. 7.

14 September

You always tend to see only the negative side of things. The whole universe is yours, but you continually complain about the lack of this, or the need for that. No, the only thing you are lacking is a divine philosophy.

I ask someone, 'Do you know what possessions you have?' and he says, 'All I have is the roof over my head.' To this I reply, 'Oh, you poor soul, you never go out, cooped up as you are in your attic. Go out and see your inheritance. You own a vast, immense estate. Come with me and see what belongs to you, all the forests, lakes, rivers and stars... Look within yourself too, and you will see that you possess riches beyond belief.* You want for nothing!' Most human beings are like the person who, up to their neck in water, complains of being thirsty. They do have water, they are in fact surrounded by an ocean, but they allow themselves to die of thirst.

* Related reading: *Golden Rules for Everyday Life,* Izvor No. 227, Chap. 10.

15 September

Your thoughts and feelings, depending on their nature and the strength you give to them, follow a predetermined path in space, before returning to the centre from which they were launched, that is, yourself. If these thoughts and feelings are pure and generous, they will return to you as blessings. If they are poisoned by the venom in your head and heart, you will soon know about it! This is what is referred to as the boomerang effect,* and it is a law that works for both good and evil.

Of course, even if you are a disciple of Initiatic Science, you will not manage to control your thoughts and feelings overnight, but the main thing is to become increasingly aware each day of the importance of this issue. After a while, not only will you be in control of your psychic life, but when strange and harmful influences try to attack you, you will be able to repel them.

* Related reading: *The Book of Divine Magic,* Izvor No. 226, Chap. 11.

16 September

Academic knowledge is useful as it greatly enriches human beings and provides them with a job, prestige, authority and money. But this knowledge will not transform them because it is superficial; it does not reach the depths of their being. You can accumulate as much knowledge about mathematics, geography, history, and so on as you like, but if you are timid, sensual, greedy and prone to anger, your learning will not change you; you will remain timid, sensual, greedy and prone to anger!

For example, no university will teach you about the hereafter or about life after death and reincarnation. So no matter how great your scientific learning, without knowledge of these essential subjects you cannot expect to have that hope, conviction or strength of will which would enable you to transform yourself. Whereas if you learned about how our souls continue to live in the other world and how they reincarnate, the revelation of these laws would make it impossible for you to remain the same, you would be compelled to become more mindful of both your outward and inner behaviour.*

* Related reading: *Man's Psychic Life: Elements and Structures,* Izvor No. 222, Chap. 7.

17 September

*E*xistence is nothing but a never-ending struggle between two antagonistic forces: life and death.* If we observe the creatures around us, we see that these two powerful adversaries are perpetually facing off, and it is always the weakness of one that gives strength to the other. When a kingdom is powerful and prosperous, its enemies keep a low profile, but when, through the neglect of its rulers or its citizens, the same kingdom starts to weaken, its enemies quickly make their presence felt and eventually destroy it.

The same phenomenon also occurs inside us, for hostile forces are always threatening to weaken us by sapping our inspiration and our courage; we must be conscious of this in order to resist it. We have come to earth to carry out some work, and must not let negative forces win. As much as we can, through knowledge, faith, hope and love, we must help to maintain life.

* Related reading: *Christmas and Easter in the Initiatic Tradition,* Izvor No. 209, Chap. 4.

268

18 September

A magus who prepares a talisman must know the relationship* that exists between physical objects, the forces of nature and the beings of the invisible world. For what is a talisman? It is an object that, due to the metal from which it is made and to the signs and characters inscribed on it, is able to absorb and retain various forces. That is why the magus links it with invisible beings, so that it may be a source of influences, either good or bad, harmonious or chaotic. But a white magus will only prepare talismans that produce beneficial influences.

The work of the magus is identical to that of nature, which fills stones, plants, animals and even human beings with a particular essence that can subsequently be used. We can thus benefit from the presence of these natural energies in all things, but we must be aware of the laws and always make use of these energies for the good of all.

* Related reading: *A Philosophy of Universality,* Izvor No. 206, Chap. 3.

19 September

*T*here is a branch of physics that studies the strength of materials, as it is very important when building housing, dams, bridges, tunnels and so on, to know how these materials will react to pressure, vibrations, shock and wear. The aim of this research is to find out which materials are the strongest and the best suited to the conditions to which they will be subjected.

In the same way, Initiatic Science accords great importance to the strength of those materials you will use to build within yourselves something strong enough to withstand winds, floods and earthquakes; in other words, those internal trials and tribulations to which you will be inescapably exposed. The strongest materials are those you gain through the practice of the virtues of goodness, fairness, purity and wisdom. Cosmic Intelligence condemns all matter not enlightened by the Deity to rapid disintegration.* You can build a resilient body only by using materials infused with divine strength.

* Related reading: *Light is a Living Spirit,* Izvor No. 212, Chap. 7.

20 September

Analyze yourself and you will notice that whenever you form a relationship or an association of some sort, you are guided by your instinctive likes or dislikes rather than by your reasoning. Good sense comes later, when things start to go wrong or you feel let down. But by then it is too late.

When a man and a woman decide to become a couple, what is it that motivates them? Sympathy and attraction. It is only later, when they realize they were mistaken about each other, that they start to use their reason. And the same goes for dislikes. If you do not like someone, you avoid them or set yourself against them. Then one day, you discover quite by chance that this person for whom you had such antipathy is actually far more honest, reliable and brave than the person you liked so much originally. So, be careful, do not rely too much on your likes and dislikes. Let reason have its say from the very beginning.*

* Related reading: *The Seeds of Happiness,* Izvor No. 231, Chap. 2.

21 September

A blind man and a man with no legs were brought before the judge one day, accused of stealing all the fruit from an apple tree. The legless man said to the judge, 'But sir, how could I do such a thing, when I have no legs?' And the blind man said, 'How could I be guilty when I can't see a thing?' This left everyone very perplexed until suddenly someone in the audience, a bit more clever than the rest, called out, 'If the man with no legs stands on the blind man's shoulders, together they can pick all the fruits from the tree!' And of course this was how it had happened. The blind man carried the legless man, and the legless man, who could see perfectly clearly, said, 'More to the left or the right, forward a bit, back a bit.'

Well, the man without legs represents the intellect, perched on the shoulders of the blind man, the heart. The heart with its feelings, desires and wishes, is below. The brain, the mind, which is above, steers the tandem so that together they achieve their goal. This is how the heart and mind* work together to commit crimes or to carry out good deeds, depending on whether or not they are enlightened by the soul and the spirit.

* Related reading: *Cosmic Balance, The Secret of Polarity,* Izvor No. 237, Chap. 11.

22 September

Let's suppose that you are assailed by wicked thoughts or feelings of jealousy, bitterness and ill will, and no matter what you do, you cannot shake them off. What should you do? Begin by taking a quiet look at these evil forces and beings. Notice what form they take, and how they scheme. Just by observing them, you are already placing yourself above them, and this is what happens: when they sense that someone is watching them, it bothers them. And if you then cast a few rays of light on them, they will scatter as they cannot bear light. Obviously, they may return, in fact they certainly will, but you must simply continue to watch them and project a beam of light on them until finally you manage to get rid of them for good. Yes, because you will have succeeded in always remaining above them.*

* Related reading: *A New Earth – Methods, Exercises, Formulas, Prayers,* Complete Works, Vol. 13, Chap. 5.

23 September

What misleads human beings is the fact that the consequences of their thoughts and actions are not immediate. When they give in to their chaotic feelings, or do something reprehensible, they see no disastrous results and they feel just the same as before and sometimes even better.

Why has the Lord arranged things in this way? To give human beings the time and the opportunity to see the error of their ways and make amends. Instead of raining blows down on us immediately, cosmic love gives us a breathing space in which to put our affairs to rights and lead a better life. If you break a civil law by cheating on your income tax for instance, it takes a few months or even years before the taxman catches up with you. Meanwhile you still have time to mend your mistakes. The same thing applies to your inner life: the chance that is given us to revise and correct our mistakes is an aspect of cosmic love.*

* Related reading: *The Seeds of Happiness,* Izvor No. 231, Chap. 10.

24 September

Each seed receives the elements it needs from the tree that produced it so that once planted, it is able to grow and become a tree like its parent. In appearance, the seed is different from the tree but on a more subtle plane, the image of the tree is inscribed within it. This is why, given good soil, the right temperature, water and light, the seed will eventually resemble the tree in every way.

This symbol of the seed helps us to understand the passage from *Genesis*, which says that God created man *'in his own image, after his likeness'*. Humans are seeds whose destiny is one day to resemble the Cosmic Tree from which they fell. This is why all our efforts should be concentrated on consciously drawing nearer to the image of our heavenly Father that we carry within us, and to vibrate in unison with Him in order to be like Him.*

* Related reading: *The True Meaning of Christ's Teaching,* Izvor No. 215, Chap. 3.

25 September

What an extraordinary adventure the ear of wheat has! First, it is harvested then it is tied into sheaves, threshed and sent to the mill to be ground between two huge stones. When it has been reduced to flour, it is mixed with water, kneaded into a dough, and put in a blazing oven to bake. Just when it might think that all its troubles are over, along comes someone with a knife to cut it into slices, and then people sink their teeth into it and chew it.

There is a lot to be learned from the life of an ear of wheat, and it is well worth thinking carefully about it, as a person's own evolution* follows the same process. All of us have to undergo many ordeals before we are finally moulded, like wheat, into something fit to be offered in sacrifice for the salvation of humanity.

* Related reading: *The Seeds of Happiness,* Izvor No. 231, Chap. 10.

26 September

*O*ur teaching contains everything you need to solve your problems and overcome your difficulties and sorrows. The only problem is that you do not realize it. After hearing or reading my lectures you say, 'Oh how beautiful, how magnificent. I feel wonderful, uplifted!' and you look no further than these feelings of joy and wonder. You never really register anything in order to apply it to your own life.

Feelings, sensations, joy and pleasure always take precedence. Such an attitude is detrimental not only to the spiritual life, for even if you spend your life travelling, reading, and going to concerts, the theatre or to museums, you will remain ignorant, feeble and wretched. Whenever you get the chance to do something enjoyable or pleasurable, always try to see what you can learn from it* – this is the quintessence of wisdom.

* Related reading: *Life and Work in an Initiatic School - Training for the Divine,* Complete Works, Vol. 30, Chap. 2.

27 September

It is up to each of you to decide to work for the collectivity rather than just for yourself. It is in your own interest to do so, for you are a part of that collectivity, and when the collectivity makes progress and things get better, you also benefit. You benefit because you have placed your capital in a bank known as the human family, a universal brotherhood of which you are a member. Whereas, when you work for yourself, for your own very limited little self, nothing good can come of it. 'Yes it will, since I have worked for myself', you might say. No, your egotistical, individual self is a bottomless pit, and by working for that alone, you have thrown everything into this pit. You should work for another, much higher goal – the ideal of universality.*

* Related reading: *'In Spirit and in Truth'*, Izvor No. 235, Chap. 17.

28 September

You have still not understood why the brain is situated at the top of the body. If you had understood, instead of always staying below on the level of the heart, instead of suffering and weeping and drowning in your emotions when you are in difficulties, you would force yourself to rise to the level of reason, intelligence and light.

When sorrow* or disappointment make you feel like crying, say to yourself, 'Very well, a few tears, if you insist. Let me get my handkerchief ready. But wait, first, I must think on things.' So you think it over, and in doing so you find a solution much sooner than if you had given way to your emotions. If you do not do this, you will weep and wail for hours – until sheer exhaustion forces you to stop – and the next day your tears will start all over again. But tears and lamentations solve nothing. Instead of always being concerned with your feelings, why not move to the spiritual region of pure reason, pure wisdom and pure light?

* Related reading: *The Path of Silence,* Izvor No. 229, Chap. 3.

29 September

Study the two pillars of the Tree of Life: mercy and severity.* In order to succeed and be useful, a teacher must know how to work with both – sometimes with leniency, sometimes with severity.

A Master must be capable of showing a great deal of love and tenderness, but he must also be strict when the progress and advancement of his disciples require it. And if his disciples do not accept this severity, they should not be in an Initiatic School. A Master needs workers for heaven, but if they can think of nothing but their own little personalities, and are always getting upset, they are useless. True disciples must put their own personality aside, and show themselves to be all spirit, all intelligence. Only then can the Master count on them for divine work.

* Related reading: *The Faith that Moves Mountains,* Izvor No. 238, Chap. 10.

30 September

Some doctrines from India teach us that the world is an illusion, 'maya'. No. The world is a reality – not the reality, but a reality. And matter is also a reality. What is truly an illusion, the most detrimental illusion humans have, is this belief that we are separate from universal life,* from that unique Being whose existence fills the whole of space, but whom we can neither see nor understand because our lower self stands in the way.

This is therefore the aim of our meditation and prayers: to detach ourselves from this restrictive lower self and draw nearer to our higher Self, which dwells in infinity, eternity and fulfilment. Once the communication is established, we can journey freely to our higher Self, our cosmic Self, which vibrates in harmony with all beings.

* Related reading: *Man's Two Natures: Human and Divine,* Izvor No. 213, Chap. 3.

1 October

Someone who remains silent shows that they are ready to listen and thus to obey. On the other hand, someone who speaks up shows that they want to take the initiative, to lead and to dominate. Silence is therefore characteristic of the feminine principle, which submits to and models itself on the masculine principle.

The reason we must learn to re-establish silence within us is so the divine Spirit can work on us. As long as we are rebellious, stubborn and anarchic, the Spirit cannot guide us and we remain weak and miserable. As soon as we manage to be silent, we place ourselves in the hands of the Spirit, which guides us toward the divine world.*

* Related reading: *The Path of Silence,* Izvor No. 229, Chap. 8.

2 October

Eating is a process by which we introduce materials into our organism that will contribute to the building not only of our physical body, but of our subtle bodies as well. So, it is particularly important to carry out this act – which we repeat every day, several times a day – in a state of peace and harmony. This is why I always stress the importance of meditating for a few minutes before meals.

I know that this is not a very widespread habit, and that most people do not even say a prayer: they instantly pounce on the food, swallowing it while talking, squabbling and clattering the cutlery. That is why they obtain no great benefits from food; they absorb only its crude elements. In order to absorb the subtle, etheric elements of our food, we must prepare ourselves to eat it in a harmonious and meditative state.*

* Related reading: *The Path of Silence,* Izvor No. 229, Chap. 4.

3 October

*O*ften when I speak to you, something inside you rebels and you think, 'But doesn't the Master see the difficult conditions we live in?' Yes, I see them; that is all I see everywhere. But I also see other things; I see the good conditions that exist, which you do not see for you are so fixated on the difficulties that you are blind to the rest. And what I see above all, are the good conditions you have within you, the treasures and wonderful riches, whereas you see only the outer situation.

When you understand me, you will feel stronger and richer. Yes, you always need someone who encourages you. You see only your weaknesses and your poverty, while there are so many other things to see!*

* Related reading: *What is a Spiritual Master?*, Izvor No. 207, Chap. 6.

4 October

*H*uman beings are free only when they succeed in re-establishing true hierarchy within themselves.* When they do so, they are kings; they regain their place on the throne and everything – their feelings, thoughts, instincts and desires – obeys them. For most people, freedom means opening a door and leaving, claiming, 'I'm free', even though they carry all their prisons within them. No, those who give priority to their desires, whims and passions are slaves, and their desire to be free is quite misplaced. In reality, only the spirit is free. So only those who are governed by the spirit, that is to say, by the light, by all that is noble, great and just, have the right to be free.

* Related reading: *Freedom, the Spirit Triumphant,* Izvor No. 211, Chap. 1.

5 October

*H*uman beings rarely know how to emerge from their self-centredness in order to do something for others. Of course, their education is often to blame. Parents tell their children, 'Don't be so stupid, don't always make the first move, let others come looking for you!' Yes, that is true, but people will only look for them if they are useful. If someone is a baker, for example, people will seek him out to get bread. To be sought after, you must always have something to give. If you do not give anything, if you are closed-off and icy, who will come to seek you out?

Human beings like only that which is alive, warm and radiant; they avoid whatever is dull and lifeless. Look at a rose in bloom – it produces a delightful fragrance and everyone comes to smell it, even bees and butterflies draw near, because it has opened up. So, why remain closed, without fragrance?*

* Related reading: *Golden Rules for Everyday Life*, Izvor No. 227, Chap. 93.

6 October

It is said that there is strength in unity, but more often than not, this unity is understood externally, in the social, political and military domains: people unite to build or unite to destroy, but it is always an external unity.

From now on, we must understand unity internally; we must be united by our ideal, we must be united by a divine idea, united by our brotherly love, united in the work we do to bring about the kingdom of God. Then, yes, unity becomes an extraordinary power. There is nothing wrong with external unity, but it is incomplete: people associate for a while and then their association comes to an end and everyone goes back to their own affairs. Whereas the unity of which we speak, the unity that is true strength, lasts forever.

7 October

Learn to move objects lovingly and you will feel that the harmony of your gestures is reflected within you. People seldom realize that the way they do things influences their inner state. But try to be aware of this, and the day you feel angry or agitated, tell yourself that this is the time to practise. Then take an object, give it a few light and gentle strokes – you will immediately feel that you are transforming something within you, that you are changing the currents.

You must learn to change your states. When you are troubled or stressed, why should it last all day long? Stop and say, 'Today, I feel as if I might tear myself apart, I must give a different rhythm to my gestures and my words' and then do so – you have the methods.*

* Related reading: *The Book of Divine Magic,* Izvor No. 226, Chap. 17.

8 October

*O*ne of people's greatest misfortunes is that they do not know what attitude they should adopt towards their weaknesses and flaws. The greater our flaw, the more frightened and humiliated we are, the more we are daunted by it. However, it should be just the opposite. Who created this flaw? We ourselves, whether consciously or not. This flaw is the fruit of our ill will, our dark desires or our lack of knowledge. At first, this flaw was tiny – a negative thought or feeling that we kept inside and nurtured – then it snowballed into something bigger, it became a mountain, a vice we can no longer get rid of.

In any case, we are its creator. The greater the vice, the greater the proof of our strength, since it is we who have given it the power it manifests. And so, if it derives its power from us, why shouldn't we be able to strip it of that power?*

* Related reading: *True Alchemy or the Quest for Perfection,* Izvor No. 221, Chap. 1.

9 October

Contemplating Isis unveiled: this is the culmination of the Initiate's journey. By means of their purity and wisdom, Initiates bring down the veils of Isis, of nature, one by one, so that they can behold her in all her manifestations, know her every secret, know her in all her beauty and light.

This is why, symbolically, ideally, a woman who stands disrobed before her beloved represents Isis unveiled before the eyes of the Initiate. Human beings, understanding nothing of this, have desecrated everything, but the fact is that throughout their lives, they unknowingly repeat the mysteries of initiation, the mysteries of Isis. Why must the bride, who is covered in veils, reveal herself on her wedding night to her beloved so that he may behold her? Almost no one understands the profound, underlying reason for these customs anymore, and that is a pity. This is why you at least should try to prepare yourselves to approach one of the greatest mysteries of nature: Isis unveiled.*

* Related reading: *The Living Book of Nature,* Izvor No. 216, Chap. 7.

10 October

When you think of helping someone, of comforting and soothing them, your thoughts go swirling around them like little angels to the rescue. What a pity that no one sees them, neither the person who sends these thoughts, nor the one who receives them!* It is true that it is certainly better not to see everything that goes on in the invisible world. Why? Because human beings, who are unable to nurture good thoughts and feelings for very long, much less rein them in when they are bad, are always out there destroying and murdering each other with their thoughts. And so, what a sight! A woman would like to get rid of her husband. She has never dared to, but many times, by means of her thoughts, she has formed little assassins to carry out her plan!

Fortunately, for the most part, human beings do not know the secret of materialization of thought, for you can be sure that they would use it more often for evil than for good.

* Related reading: *The Powers of Thought,* Izvor No. 224, Chap. 11.

11 October

When you are tired, sick or discouraged, think of the light that is disseminated throughout the universe. Concentrate on it and imagine that you are letting it flow within you: it will eliminate the impure elements throughout your body and you will feel regenerated and able to expend great energy. The most effective way to take in this light is to give thanks to the Lord and bless His name. That is why you should get into the habit of repeating several times a day, 'Thank you, thank you, Lord, thank you for life, thank you for the light. May your name be blessed for all eternity.'*

* Related reading: *The Seeds of Happiness,* Izvor No. 231, Chap. 8.

12 October

*I*deally, we should possess both form and force, that is to say, matter and spirit. It is bad to crystalize yourself in matter, because events will break you. However, if you abandon matter to live only in the spirit, it may be wonderful, but you will have to go and live in the next world – which is not recommended.

The ideal is to achieve a fusion of form and spirit: to protect the form so that it is not broken by spiritual forces, while keeping the fire of the spirit alive so that the form may be constantly animated. All the materialists who cling to the form will be swept away by cosmic currents. All the civilizations, all the religions that are stuck in their old forms will be broken by the surging powers of renewal. Everything must be renewed; there is no shelter on earth for that which refuses to evolve.*

* Related reading: *The Faith that Moves Mountains,* Izvor No. 238, Chap. 8.

13 October

*E*verything in today's culture primarily revolves around the needs of the physical body. But to be so concerned with satisfying the physical body is dangerous, for the body is vulnerable, perishable, and founding a culture on something that is destined to disappear so quickly has deplorable consequences for all that human beings do. Their reasoning and behaviour will necessarily be flawed because they are based on the wrong premise.

Whereas if people strive to satisfy the needs of the soul and the spirit, which are not bound by the laws of time and space, everything they do will bear the mark of light and immortality. This will be the coming of the kingdom of God. If people currently manifest so little greatness and nobility, it is because they are dominated by their physical body. They must free themselves from it, and now place the soul and the spirit at the heart of their philosophy.*

* Related reading: *Freedom, the Spirit Triumphant*, Izvor No. 211, Chap. 3.

14 October

*P*arents should stop being upset when they see their children struggling a little to do what is asked of them. Children are so resourceful and resilient that they forget these little hardships very quickly; what will stay with them is the meaning of effort, which will help to shape their character. This is what should make parents happy. If, on the contrary, parents say, 'Oh, the poor thing! He mustn't suffer and be sad', to spare the child a little grief, they will make him lazy, weak, selfish and capricious. Such is the love and pedagogy of adults!

Parents need to realize that on the pretext of not wanting to let their children suffer, they often foster their faults. That is why parents must change their attitude, otherwise they will be responsible for hindering their children's evolution and they will suffer.*

* Related reading: *Love Greater Than Faith,* Izvor No. 239, Chap. 4.

15 October

Attuning yourselves means to send a smile, a loving gaze, a rocket of love, missiles of love to all the luminous creatures in space, saying to them, 'Oh, you, who inhabit immensity, I love you, I understand you, I am in harmony with you!'

You do not yet know how much you can do with your love. You are content to focus it on a few earthly creatures, and of course, it is not wrong to direct your thoughts, feelings and gaze towards human beings, but this is very limited, and you cannot even be sure that they will benefit from it. Whereas if you send your love to the sublime entities, where no one may have noticed that something was sent into space, these entities on the contrary receive it, rejoice and send this love back to you a hundredfold. These are true exchanges, true communion – fusion with the universal Soul.*

* Related reading: *The Path of Silence,* Izvor No. 229, Chap. 7

16 October

Love organizes and harmonizes everything within you and around you. This is a truth that most people do not consider; and that is why they are always discontented, agitated and bitter, and do not succeed at anything they undertake.

Love... who cares about love? Apart from sexual love, it is always relegated to last place. We ask ourselves, 'Love – what does it mean to love? And what should we love?' Everything. To love, truly, does not mean to feel an attraction for a man or a woman. To love is to be inhabited by love.* It is then possible to achieve everything in life: we become more capable, more penetrating and more lucid. This state of love prepares the conditions for the best manifestations.

* Related reading: *The Book of Revelation: a Commentary,* Izvor No. 230, Chap. 17, Part 3.

17 October

*G*ardeners who have failed to sow a crop do not revolt when they see none growing. They simply say to themselves, 'It's only natural, old thing – since you didn't have time to sow carrots, you have no carrots, but you can have lettuce, parsley and onions because these you did sow.'

Yes, when it comes to fruits and vegetables, human beings are very knowledgeable, but when it comes to the realm of the soul or thought, they know nothing: they believe they will reap happiness, joy and peace, even as they sow violence, cruelty and wickedness. Well no, they will inevitably reap violence, cruelty and wickedness. However, as they do not understand this, they revolt against what is happening to them. Well, this proves that they are not good farmers. If they were enlightened, reasonable and prudent, if they watched over themselves so as not to sow, plant and propagate dark and destructive influences with their words, thoughts, writings or any other means, their destiny would improve.*

* Related reading: *Man, Master of his Destiny,* Izvor No. 202, Chap. 1.

18 October

We are used to considering heaven and earth as two separate and even foreign or opposite realities. In fact, no, they are continually in contact with each other; otherwise, nothing can be explained. Heaven and earth... or even more simply, the sun and the earth: there is a constant stream of exchanges between them and it is these exchanges that produce life. We perceive very little of these exchanges at the moment. We see the sun's rays beaming down upon us, but we do not see what also rises up from the earth towards the sun. Only clairvoyants have seen these beings who descend from the higher regions to work on the plants and stones, and then return to heaven once their work is done.

Extraordinarily beautiful and poetic literature has been written on this subject, and one day you too will be able to contemplate these creatures coming and going between the earth and the sun, and even further away.*

* Related reading: *The Living Book of Nature,* Izvor No. 216, Chap. 4, Part 3.

19 October

A human being, as a microcosm that reflects the macrocosm, is the repository of the entire memory of the world. Human beings possess within themselves the archives of the universe, archives that are also represented symbolically in the Tree of Life by the sephirah *Daath**, Knowledge. *Daath* is original matter, the primordial matter over which God breathed in the beginning of the world in order to fertilize it. Since matter is the substance of Creation, it is able to hold memory. And the Spirit awakens this memory by moving lightly over matter just as the wind makes the strings of an Aeolian harp vibrate.

---

* Daath is only rarely mentioned in the Kabbalah. This eleventh sephirah is traditionally located on the central pillar of the Tree of Life, between *Tiphareth* and *Kether*. (See Volume 10 of the Complete Works, Chapter 17 "Day and Night").

20 October

When an instructor, a Master, sees that he is unable to make human beings wiser, he does not fuss or worry, for he knows that he has a great helper and ally: life. Since there is nothing the Master can do, life takes charge and gives those who are recalcitrant a few shakes.

Unfortunately, human beings do not necessarily discover the truth by being shaken up, because life explains nothing. It delivers knocks, strikes them down and pummels them without giving an explanation. If they want explanations, they must seek out a Master. Together, the Master and life will educate them. When I see that I am not succeeding in enlightening someone and making them wiser, I call upon life and say, 'Listen, take care of this one for me because they are hard-headed'. 'Understood', says life. And once life has given them a few hard knocks, as they do not understand why, life sends them back to me so that I can enlighten them.*

* Related reading: *What is a Spiritual Master?*, Izvor No. 207, Chap. 6.

21 October

In order to devote one's entire life to the Lord from a young age, a disciple must already have worked a great deal towards this during their previous incarnations. Otherwise, it is impossible. Even if you want to, you cannot, because your being does not vibrate, does not rejoice, is not inspired by this idea of devoting yourself to God; it simply does not appeal – on the contrary, it even frightens you.

It is not possible for everyone to accept such a commitment. Even if, theoretically, philosophically, we understand the splendour of such an ideal, in practice, we cannot realize it because our whole being strains in other directions: there are other needs, other desires and other pleasures. For most of you, it is therefore very difficult to dedicate your life to a sublime ideal, but it is not too late to begin working towards it.*

* Related reading: *'Walk While You Have the Light'*, Izvor No. 244, Chap. 12.

22 October

For many people, even very cultured ones, poetry is but a string of vague, bizarre, disjointed expressions or images that do not correspond to the symbolic language of nature. As these people lack criteria and also tend to dwell in these hazy regions, they are dazzled and sink even deeper into these regions.

True poetry is the Word, the divine Word in which all the elements are linked together by secret correspondences. True poetry awakens in humans the sense that they have already lived a divine life on high, and sets their most spiritual chords vibrating. So, if a poem does not stir this kind of emotion in you, if it does not awaken in you any reminiscence of Paradise, if it merely offers you a few vague, mild sensations, you can be sure that it is not true poetry.*

* Related reading: *Creation: Artistic and Spiritual,* Izvor No. 223, Chap. 3.

23 October

Art will save the world, but only art that is conscious and enlightened by the truths of Initiatic Science. In future, artists will be given pride of place, for a true artist is also an interpreter of philosophy and religion.*

Being an artist means realizing on the physical plane what the mind perceives as right and true, and what the heart feels is good, so that the higher world, the world of the spirit may descend to manifest itself in matter. A perfect artist is one who has successfully established order and reason in their thoughts, and brought peace and love into their heart, so that everything they do is beautiful and harmonious.

---

* Related reading: *Creation: Artistic and Spiritual,* Izvor No. 223, Chap. 1.

24 October

In Hebrew, God's name is made up of four letters: *Yod He Vav He* יהוה These four letters correspond to the four principles within a human being: *Yod,* the spirit; *He,* the soul; *Vav,* the intellect; and the second *He,* the heart. But for these four principles to manifest themselves and incarnate, a fifth is needed: *Shin* ש ; symbol of the union between spirit and matter, which is interposed between them at the centre. יהוה becomes יהשוה , that is, *Yeshua,* which is Jesus' name in Hebrew. In this way, by proclaiming himself and by proclaiming all human beings sons and daughters of God, by asking them to work for the realization of the kingdom of God on earth, Jesus was simply insisting on human beings' true mission: to incarnate the Deity. Jesus Christ is the Word made flesh. By enveloping Himself in flesh, God became human. Man and woman are but the physical manifestation of the Deity.*

* Related reading: *The Symbolic Language of Geometrical Figures,* Izvor No. 218, Chap. 4.

25 October

Human beings need to see, to hear, to meet people, and even to receive shocks and to suffer, because they are so inert, numb and stagnant that if they do not receive stimulation from the outside world, if they are not roused and shaken up, they will do nothing.

That is why we need instructors and Masters so much. Thanks to the life they lead, to their vibrations, to their very pure and luminous thoughts, these beings manage to stir something within us. And if they do not always succeed, it is not because they are incapable or weak, but because we have allowed ourselves to be buried beneath too many layers of lifeless, leaden material.*

* Related reading: *What is a Spiritual Master?*, Izvor No. 207, Chap. 6.

26 October

There is no such thing as impurity, ugliness or evil to the universal spirit. To the cosmic spirit, the universe is a harmony in which there is no dissonance. Of course, when you look at the world from the earth's perspective, not everything is perfectly beautiful or good. But when you look down from a great height to see immensity, everything changes.

When you are cooking a meal, and you are chopping and mixing the ingredients, if these ingredients were conscious, they would say that you were cruel, unfair and unmerciful for making them suffer like that. But as you see things differently, you do not feel guilty, you simply say, 'I am preparing a dish that everyone will enjoy'.

27 October

When you want to pray and link yourself with God, imagine a living, radiant centre somewhere in space towards which all the beings of light converge. From this centre, you see rays of light streaming out in all directions to nourish living creatures. This image will direct your thoughts exactly towards the place where the divine presence is the most intense, and your prayer will be met with results.

All the great Masters and Initiates concentrate on this point, which is a centre of light, and their thoughts generate such power in space that a disciple who practises every day receives infinite blessings from this power.

28 October

*T*he soul needs infinite space,* and when it feels restricted and suffocated, it seeks to escape by any means possible. Alcohol and drugs are among these means because they have the ability to drive the soul out of the physical body and thus give it, if only briefly, the illusion of freedom and space. But this is not a solution, because drugs are ultimately chemical substances given to the body. However, the need for escape comes from the soul not the body. Drugs are a sign that the soul is seeking to travel in infinite space, but drugs cannot satisfy the soul and, not only can they not satisfy it, but they destroy the body. That is why I do not advise anyone to use them, under any pretext whatsoever. Joy, dilation, freedom and fulfilment are to be sought by spiritual means.

* Related reading: *Under the Dove, the Reign of Peace,* Izvor No. 208, Chap. 9.

29 October

Most human beings are convinced that wanting to do good at all times is foolish, and that intelligent people try to fend for themselves, even if it is at the expense of others, or to seek revenge on those who have harmed them.* Initiates, on the other hand, believe that goodness represents the fruits of man and that if humans have come down to earth, it is precisely in order to bear fruit. These fruits are the luminous thoughts, warm feelings, noble deeds, and the joy, beauty and peace that we bring to others.

We must get up every morning with the thought of doing good. The seeds, the little sprouts that God has placed in our soul will then begin to come out, they will become confident and in a very short while, they will bear flowers and fruits.

* Related reading: *Cosmic Balance, The Secret of Polarity,*
Izvor No. 237, Chap. 12.

30 October

When you are unhappy, do not just sit there doing nothing, try to extricate yourself from this state of darkness by turning on all the inner lamps the Creator has placed within you – all sorts of lamps: big, small, in every colour. For there is an electric current flowing to light them, a current that comes from far away... from the cosmic powerhouse, God Himself.

But you never think of turning on your lamps. You will say, 'And how do we light them?' It is very simple: in the physical world, you have a button or a switch that you have to turn or press. In the psychic world, all you need is thought to turn them on: you concentrate on the light while thinking that you are lighting lamps throughout the whole of your being, and there you have it! As soon as some of them are alight, do not stop, keep on going, still others will light up and in the end, the illumination will be fantastic.

31 October

Nature works with moisture and heat, but it knows how to apportion them. It provides moisture to make fruit grow, but if it gives too much, they rot. So, it sends heat, which dries and ripens the fruit; but if the heat is too intense, everything will be dried out and scorched, and there will be no fruit either. Nature uses moisture and heat in turn; it measures and gives them out in the right doses, and the fruits ripen!

Why don't human beings do the same in their own lives? If they asked themselves questions, if they tried to understand why they are unhappy, why they are misunderstood by their spouse, children, boss or neighbours, perhaps they would discover that there is something in them that needs to be sorted out, something that is not quite right. They are either lacking firmness or gentleness, they are too violent or too soft. Problems will resolve themselves when people figure out how to adjust, measure and apportion the elements properly, the way nature does, and then there will be an abundance of fruit – joy, happiness and harmony – all around them.*

* Related reading: *The Book of Revelation: a Commentary,* Izvor No. 230, Chap. 6.

1 November

*M*any people complain that they are obsessed, tormented, and on the verge of losing their minds. This is simply because they have come in contact with regions infested by the inferior entities that are enemies of humanity, and these entities are attacking them. Such people put up a struggle, of course, but as they are not strong enough to shake off their enemies, their struggle ends in defeat. They must find other ways of defending themselves. When a bird pecking at seeds on the ground sees a cat come along, what does the bird do? Does it wait and fight it out? No, it flies away. But human beings still do not understand what birds have always understood. Instead of taking flight, they stay and fight and, of course, they end by being stripped bare and massacred.

You will say, 'But how can I fly away?' There are so many ways! You can use your willpower or your imagination; you can pray, or read or listen to music; you can invoke the memory of a luminous moment in your life, and so forth. There are so many possibilities to choose from. The real question is whether you have the will to free yourself. No, you just sit and do nothing about it except stuff yourself with pills and pester others with accounts of your anxieties and nightmares. It is time you put an end to this negative situation by learning to fly away.*

* Related reading: *The Seeds of Happiness,* Izvor No. 231, Chap. 10.

2 November

Someone comes to see me and complains that nothing is going right for him, that he is discouraged, disappointed, and so forth. I look at him and simply tell him, 'That is because you have enrolled in the school of weakness.' 'What school is that?'* Seeing that he does not understand, I explain: 'Well, in the school of weakness, you never do any exercises to build up your strength and learn to face up to difficulties. You loaf about in armchairs, in comfort and idleness. This is all very nice, but what happens then? The result is that your inner mechanism slows down, the intensity of your life, your thoughts and your spirit gradually diminishes, and when problems and trials arise, you immediately break down. It is now time to enrol in the school of strength; that is to say, you must strive to maintain an inner state of activity, vigilance, dynamic energy, enthusiasm and courage. Knowing that the two great principles of life and death are locked in an eternal struggle, you must not give in; you must not allow negative forces to invade you and shackle you.'

* Related reading: *The Powers of Thought,* Izvor No. 224, Chap. 7.

3 November

*T*he love of many human beings is like a smoky stove that coats their inner being with soot. When the stove is alight, the windows are all closed, and the lack of air saps their vitality and makes them sluggish. But when the sun, spiritual love, comes out, the windows are thrown open to let in the fresh air, and they begin to revive. You should no longer rely so much on your stove, that is to say, on your lusts, passions, instincts and desires, for they oppose all that is most vital within you by keeping the windows of your soul closed and preventing the fresh air from entering.

You need not be afraid that you will die of boredom if you base your life on moderation and reason. No, the day the sun of wisdom and divine love begins to shine upon you, you will see that the gratification of your passions, which once mattered so much to you, has gradually come to mean nothing. Your inner sanctum will become luminous and pure, and you will know true happiness.*

* Related reading: *The Mysteries of Fire and Water,* Izvor No. 232, Chap. 14.

4 November

*E*verything is magic: a conversation, a look, all your gestures, nutrition, love, a stroll outside – everything. Many people are horrified by the mere mention of the word magic. They do not realize that they are constantly practising magic. Whether they know it or not, all they do is magic. In fact, it would be true to say that magic is the only science and that it encompasses all others: alchemy, astrology and the Cabbalah are simply branches of the science of magic.

Yes, everything is magic. For example, when you look at someone in a certain way or kiss them, you unleash formidable magical forces, and very often you play with these forces without realizing that you could set everything ablaze with them. It is as though you amused yourself by tossing lighted matches in all directions – and everything goes up in flames! So it is that many people who hate to hear any mention of magic spend most of their time playing the sorcerer's apprentice.*

* Related reading: *The Book of Divine Magic,* Izvor No. 226, Chap. 10.

5 November

Suppose you have eaten too much. No law of society will condemn you, no police officer will come and arrest you, but you will be ill in bed. What kind of justice strikes you down and puts you to bed? The laws of nature are not those of human beings. Human beings will come to visit you at your bedside and sympathize with you: 'Poor dear, we're sorry you're ill!' Yes, but they will not be able to do anything for you. Only nature can help. Obey its laws once again, and you will be cured.

You must learn which laws are the laws of nature, the divine laws to which your mind, your heart and your physical body are subject. Remember that everything you say and do means an expenditure of energy, and you must see where your energies go and take care that they do not cause any damage.*

* Related reading: *Freedom, the Spirit Triumphant,* Izvor No. 211, Chap. 8.

6 November

Nature impels people to seek pleasure, for without it life would lose its flavour, its meaning and become dull and monotonous. It is pleasure that animates and lends colour to life, so there is no question of doing away with it. The only thing is that it must not become a priority, a goal in life; rather, this natural inclination for pleasure must be used constructively.

A human being is like a ship sailing on the ocean of life. There are sailors on board who stoke the boilers so that the ship can keep moving, and at the helm is the captain, who keeps the ship on course with the help of a compass. The stokers are our instincts and appetites. They cannot see, but they provide the power to keep us moving. And the captain is our intelligence, the wisdom at the helm that steers our ship in the right direction and makes sure that it does not founder on the rocks or collide with another ship. So, keep a close eye on this ship of which you are the captain, and be sure that the crew is never left to its own devices!*

* Related reading: *The Seeds of Happiness,* Izvor No. 231, Chap. 2.

7 November

*P*eople who have great material riches are never at peace; they are constantly in a whirl of activity and worries of all kinds, always on their guard against the ambitions of dishonest, greedy people who have an eye on their fortune. And however vigilant they are, can they ever be sure of foreseeing and parrying every threat? The weight of their never-ending cares drags them more deeply into matter and cuts them off from the regions of the spirit. As a result, they waste a great deal of time and energy which could be used so much more profitably for their own evolution and that of all those whom they could have helped with their spiritual riches.

Whatever tasks you have to fulfil, it is better not to overburden yourself but be content to have just what you need. You only complicate things by asking for more.*

* Related reading: *The Seeds of Happiness,* Izvor No. 231, Chap. 5.

8 November

Do you want to show how intelligent you are? Well, it is simple: you prove that you are intelligent if you know how to overcome the inconveniences that are inherent in the life of a collectivity, if you are able to restore peace wherever you go by manifesting love, patience and kindness. Stop criticizing and you will have won a tremendous victory over yourself; you will be happy when you have succeeded in establishing harmony in and around yourself.*

You have to understand that human relations are very complex; affinities and antipathies are usually determined by past incarnations. This is why you must not judge others; whatever they do is their business and they will have to answer for it one day. What is important for you is that your relations with others should allow you to evolve and make progress and be useful and beneficial to them.

* Related reading: *The Laughter of a Sage,* Izvor No. 243, Chap. 8.

9 November

Many years ago an International Bureau of Weights and Measures was established in Sevres. Why is this bureau necessary? Because people realized that if there were no standards to refer to, weights and measures would be purely arbitrary and vary from one person to the next.

But when it comes to the inner world of thoughts and opinions, human beings never wonder whether their system of weights and measures is valid. Day and night, they weigh, measure, calculate and pronounce judgement, and it never occurs to them that they might do well to have their instruments checked by a spiritual bureau of weights and measures; that is to say, by an Initiate. Instead of asking, 'What about my heart? my will? my brain? What about my tastes and preferences? Are they in order?' everyone believes themselves to be perfect, and they express their opinions about anything and everything: about love, politics, the existence of God, the meaning of life, and so on and so forth. But what are these opinions worth?*

* Related reading: *'In Spirit and in Truth',* Izvor No. 235, Chap. 2.

10 November

*E*very individual is free to do what they want, however crazy – why not? The only problem is that when you do foolish things, you are signing a pact with beings of a lower order and afterwards you are at their mercy; there is no escape. You have had a good time, you have eaten and drunk, and now it is time to pay. Of course, it is fun to run wild. It makes you feel wonderful at the time, but it is very costly. Human beings are past masters at finding agreeable activities, but they are blind to the consequences of these pleasant pastimes; they think about nothing but pleasure. Yes, but everything comes with a price, and so many ruin themselves physically and morally for the sake of a little pleasure!

11 November

It is true that nothing is more precious than friendship,* but human beings are not always interested in having a true friend; what they are looking for is an ally, someone who will approve and encourage them, even when they behave badly. Do you know many people who want their friends to be completely sincere with them and not necessarily approve of everything they do or say? Most people feel betrayed and fly into a rage at the slightest criticism. We all know that if you want to win someone's good opinion, you have to praise, flatter and approve of them. What with those who refuse to listen to the truth and those who have found that it is not in their interest to tell it, many people around us spend their time deceiving or being deceived.

Those who truly want to evolve do not lie or try to deceive others; above all, they accept their comments and criticism. In fact, if they are truly wise, they will understand that it is useful to have enemies. Why? Because enemies can help them to advance.

* Related reading: *Cosmic Creation, Union of the Masculine and Feminine,* Izvor No. 214, Chap. 6.

12 November

No part of a fruit is more important than the seed, thanks to which you can have thousands of acres of fruit trees. For nature, the essential part of a fruit is the seed; the seed or the pit is all it cares about. If nature has wrapped them in a little flesh, it is simply a way of attracting birds and people so that they will plant those seeds.

Symbolically speaking, the seed or the pit represents the spirit; the flesh represents the space of the soul in which life circulates, and the skin is the material envelope, the physical body. There is no denying that the physical body is important. It is like a flask that prevents the perfume from evaporating; it retains the soul and spirit. However, the true person is not the body, but that minute, invisible point contained somewhere inside, which thinks, loves and creates. The fact that Cosmic Intelligence allows the physical body to die and be buried proves that it attaches very little importance to it, whereas the spirit, which is immortal, is called back to the heavenly regions from which it came.*

* Related reading: *The Symbolic Language of Geometrical Figures,* Izvor No. 218, Chap. 2.

13 November

*T*he existence of Black Madonnas is linked to the alchemical secrets of the transmutation of matter. The base material, which alchemists seek to transform, is said to be black, unorganized, raw matter: chaos. The Black Madonnas are related to this original alchemical substance. This is why these statues were usually placed underground in caves or crypts, because the matter they symbolize is extracted from the primitive virgin earth; this is what the term 'black' expresses. Alchemists used to say that just as the Virgin Mary suffered when giving birth to Christ, so matter has to be cooked for a long time in fire before giving birth to the philosopher's stone.*

* Related reading: *The Philosopher's Stone in the Gospels and in Alchemy,* Izvor No. 241, Chap. 12.

14 November

*S*ome people are happy when they have time to reflect; others are happy when they can be carefree and amuse themselves. Some need a family life; others prefer solitude and celibacy. Some need to help, succour and care for their neighbour, while others need to persecute and destroy them, and so on.

This quest for happiness, which varies with each individual depending on their own particular temperament, is always a form of the quest for God; a quest that may show a lack of wisdom or of light perhaps, but which is still a quest for God. Yes, because hidden behind this notion of happiness is God. It is He who gave humans this aspiration for happiness, so that they might eventually find Him. And even if in the meantime they seek Him in ways that lead through chimneys, sewers, swamps or graveyards, in the long run, after a multitude of experiences, they will understand that they have to seek Him in the highest regions, in the form of purity and light. And there, at last, they will truly find Him.*

* Related reading: *The Seeds of Happiness,* Izvor No. 231, Chap. 14.

15 November

*E*very one of your thoughts, feelings and actions, whether good or bad, is recorded within you. It is impossible not to make a few negative, defective recordings from time to time, but at least be conscious and careful, and as soon as you realize that you have recorded something negative, react at once and try to correct the situation.

Suppose you have thought unkindly about someone, said hurtful words, or wrecked something; be aware of what you have done and put it right. At present, you will often not be able to do much, but at least do what you can. Some people do nothing, absolutely nothing, to make amends for a negative thought or action; they are not even aware of what they have done. Whereas others are conscious of what they do and want to mend their ways. Anyone can make mistakes, but we should at least realize when we have done so and work day and night to put things right instead of doing nothing.

16 November

Someone who believes they can shirk their obligations and responsibilities in order to enjoy a more pleasant life does not know the strict laws that govern destiny. A woman thinks, 'My husband is so boring; I'm going to find someone else, someone more entertaining and attractive.' So she finds that someone then leaves her first husband, who obviously suffers as a consequence. Before long, though, she may be the one to suffer even more with this second husband.

It is not absolutely forbidden to leave one's husband or wife, but you must not do so before you have resolved the first problem. Something that seems easy is in reality very difficult, and vice versa. If you choose the path of greatest difficulty, the Lord will send His angels to help you, but if you choose the easy way out, you will still have angels to accompany you, but of another kind: avenging angels.*

* Related reading: *Golden Rules for Everyday Life,* Izvor No. 227, Chap. 52.

17 November

*B*y means of meditation and prayer, make every effort to protect yourself by taking in as much light as possible. When Initiatic Science speaks of light, it is referring in fact to benevolent entities, and when those entities dwell within you, they stand in the way of the spirits of darkness. This does not mean that the light will prevent you from being tormented occasionally. Unfortunately, as long as we are on earth, we can never be entirely sheltered from attack or conflict. Even Initiates have to shield themselves. Yes, even the purest, greatest and most powerful Initiate must constantly think to protect himself by erecting a barrier of light, a circle of flames, between himself and the spirits of evil who try to attack him. And if this is so, how can people who are weak and ignorant imagine that they need no protection?*

* Related reading: *Cosmic Balance, The Secret of Polarity,* Izvor No. 237, Chap. 14.

18 November

*T*o light a candle is not the simple, insignificant act it seems, for in doing so you are making contact with the four elements. The candle, which is solid, represents earth. When you light it you have fire. Little by little, the candle melts and a tiny pool of liquid forms in the hollow, and you have 'water'. As for air, it is always there, for it is indispensable to fire. Without air the flame would go out; even if you cannot see it, its presence is revealed by the flickering motion of the flame.

So, when you light a candle, you should be aware that you are in the presence of the four fundamental elements of creation, and that you can work with them by linking yourself to the four great angels that govern them: the Angel of Fire, the Angel of Air, the Angel of Water and the Angel of Earth.*

* Related reading: *The Mysteries of Fire and Water,* Izvor No. 232, Chap. 13.

19 November

*T*hrough their experiments with special instruments, researchers have discovered a form of sensitivity in plants that makes them react to the presence of different people depending on whether they are helpful or harmful. If someone who has harmed them comes near them, they show signs of fear. This means that they also have a form of memory.

Plants are sensitive, and in their own way so are stones. If you appreciate them and touch them lovingly, they are capable of responding and revealing certain things to you, for love is a universal language that the whole of creation, all creatures, can understand. Touch a stone with love and it will immediately vibrate differently. It can even respond with love but, of course, you have to be extremely sensitive to perceive this and decipher its language. But who wants to learn the language of stones, plants or animals? Human beings have learned to read and write in every language in the world and that is very good, but the only language that is really worth knowing is the language of living nature.*

* Related reading: *The Philosopher's Stone in the Gospels and in Alchemy,* Izvor No. 241, Chap. 4.

20 November

*B*eings and things are what they are, but by means of thought, humans have the power to influence them and make them serve the cause of good or of evil. This is what magic really is. A magus is simply a being who takes an object and imparts to it a quality that it did not already possess; he transforms an object into a talisman* by taking elements of his own quintessence and introducing them into that object. Even if certain objects possess great virtues of their own, you too must add to those virtues by means of your thoughts and your love. As long as you remain inactive, as long as you do no work with your thoughts, you will never get any significant results.

* Related reading: *The Book of Divine Magic,* Izvor No. 226, Chap. 5.

21 November

When God created man, He gave him all the possibilities he needed to attain perfection. These possibilities are on the level of thought, and this is why people must get into the habit of putting their mental faculties to work every day by practising concentration, meditation and prayer.

We have all the powers we need within us but we do not know this, for nobody has ever told us. So we spend our time looking for them elsewhere, on the outside; but the only means we shall find on the outside are those that can help us to work with matter. When it comes to transforming ourselves inwardly, to working on our soul and spirit and uniting ourselves to God, the means we need can be found only inside us, in the realm of thought. This is why the disciples of an initiatic school try to study and explore the nature of man so as to awaken all the possibilities placed in them by the Creator.*

* Related reading: *Man's Psychic Life: Elements and Structures,* Izvor No. 222, Chap. 8

22 November

*M*any people think that they are justified in leading a mediocre life on the pretext that they have no special gifts or qualities and no position in society. No, this is not a valid excuse. Even the poorest of the poor are capable of reaching a higher state of consciousness and working to help, enlighten and succour all of humanity.

Some people will say, 'It's an impossible task; there are far too many people in the world and I'm so insignificant!' Obviously, you will not establish the kingdom of God on earth overnight, but if you wish for it sincerely, all your strength and energy will be aimed towards achieving it. As it is a sublime, divine work, it will begin by having an effect on you: it will elevate and ennoble you, and since every action produces a reaction, in one way or another you will have a good influence on those around you.*

* Related reading: *Light is a Living Spirit,* Izvor No. 212, Chap. 9.

*T*o make as little noise as possible is not the primary concern of most human beings – they talk loudly, shout and bang things about. It never occurs to them that such behaviour might be harmful to themselves and to others. They manifest themselves just as they are and, having a very high opinion of themselves, they naturally expect others to put up with them. Well, this is a form of selfishness that is very detrimental to one's evolution.

Yes, pay attention; be careful not to disturb others with your noise. In doing so, you will become more conscious and develop many qualities such as delicacy, sensitivity, kindness, generosity and harmony. What is more, you will be the first to benefit from it!*

* Related reading: *The Path of Silence,* Izvor No. 229, Chap. 1.

24 November

*H*ow good it would be if everybody knew how the laws of destiny worked and understood why certain misfortunes happened to them and to others, yet still persevered in the desire to help.

Some people might say, 'Why should I help them when they are only getting what they deserve?' First of all, because the efforts you make in trying to help others are never wasted; in certain circumstances, heaven will relent when it sees your sincerity. In the second place, your efforts are also of use to you, to progress. By helping others, you develop something in yourself; your generous, disinterested intentions and actions have a positive effect on you. So help others, and you too will feel better.*

* Related reading: *The Seeds of Happiness,* Izvor No. 231, Chap. 12.

25 November

*T*he majority of people are either totally expressionless and wooden as though they were half dead, or they are continually in the grip of excitement and passions, which is no better. It is time they found a third attitude, an attitude of liveliness but a harmonious, luminous liveliness.

Unfortunately, very few understand the gravity of the matter, even the members of a family. So many husbands leave their wives, or wives their husbands, because they are sick of having the same expressionless face in front of them day after day. Even if the husband is a multi-billionaire who gives his wife everything imaginable, or the wife is the best cook in the world, as neither money nor fine cooking has anything to do with true life, their partners desert them – along with their money or their cooking! Why are men and women too stupid to understand that the only thing that can satisfy a human being is life; a life that is constantly new and vibrant.*

* Related reading: *Cosmic Balance, The Secret of Polarity,* Izvor No. 237, Chap. 2.

26 November

When a wave of light is projected into space, another symmetrical ray spontaneously appears. That is to say, if the first ray follows a convex curve, the curve of the second will be concave. This shows that fullness and emptiness do not exist in themselves; they are complementary. Fullness and emptiness are the two fundamental principles, masculine and feminine, which always work together in the universe.

In human beings, these two principles are represented by the soul and the spirit, the heart and the mind. In Initiatic Science, this phenomenon is symbolized by the snake, which moves like a sine wave. Our spine, which supports the rest of our skeleton, is built on the same pattern: the sinusoidal motion of a snake, that is to say the movement of light.*

* Related reading: *The Zodiac, Key to Man and to the Universe,* Izvor No. 220, Chap. 3.

27 November

*F*eeling good or bad, happy or unhappy is quite relative. Say you find that you are a little bored and sad; life seems colourless and bland.

Suddenly you receive bad news: there has been an accident and a member of your family has been seriously injured. Then of course, you are really unhappy. A few hours later you learn that it was not true; it was a case of mistaken identity. Ah, suddenly what joy! Life seems so buoyant, beautiful and rich! Yes, but why did it not seem like that earlier? Why did it take a false alarm about a family tragedy to make you conscious of the fact that you were already happy?*

* Related reading: *The Seeds of Happiness,* Izvor No. 231, Chap. 9.

28 November

*H*uman beings are veritable pharmaceutical laboratories equipped with every kind of medicine but also with toxic substances. At the sight of certain people we sometimes say, 'Oh, what poison' or 'Here comes the plague!' whereas with others, on the contrary, scarcely have we laid eyes on them than we breathe more freely. Your sweetheart, for instance, is like a pharmacy full of all the most effective remedies. As soon as he or she appears, even if you are exhausted or ill, you get up, your eyes sparkle, and you are yourself again! Yes, the emanations of a human being contain both toxic and curative elements.

Science has never considered this question but it is a reality. There are some doctors, for example, whose mere presence has such a salutary effect on sick people that simply by taking their hand they put them on the road to recovery. People like this have truly been born to emanate healing etheric particles. This is what it means to be a true doctor.*

* Related reading: *Hrani Yoga – The Alchemical and Magical Meaning of Nutrition,* Complete Works, Vol. 16, Chap. 4, Part 3.

29 November

Many people love someone who, little by little, turns out to be dishonest, unjust and cruel, and then they are faced with a dilemma: must they make the effort to go on loving them or not? Of course, when you love someone, that love always has some beneficial effects on a subtle plane. On the other hand, it is never good to stick with someone who sets out on such a bad path. It is useless to devote so much time and energy to someone who is determined to turn their back on the light.

The only thing that matters is your love and the quality of that love, its purity and light. If you cannot love a particular man or woman, love others, love the whole world, so that the fountain of love continues to flow. What matters most is not for whom it flows, but that it should continue to flow and that it should be pure.*

* Related reading: *The Seeds of Happiness,* Izvor No. 231, Chap. 17.

30 November

When you find yourself faced with great difficulties or in a very dangerous situation, you must not give way to apprehension and anxiety. React; link yourself to divine Providence and ask for light. Thanks to the light, you will see with greater clarity and feel more peaceful, and once your heart and your head are calmer, you will be able to do what has to be done.

Every danger or obstacle the human soul has to face can be summed up in two words, fear and darkness, and you must do everything possible to overcome them. There is only one legitimate fear that you must not only tolerate but welcome and that is the fear of disrupting the divine order of things. If you are still afraid of hunger and thirst, of public opinion, of dying of illness or in an accident, you are not yet a disciple. The one thing a disciple fears is to break the divine laws.*

* Related reading: *True Alchemy or the Quest for Perfection,* Izvor No. 221, Chap. 5.

1 December

You cannot be safe and secure unless you give everything to the Lord: your spirit, your soul, your body – everything, even your family, your house and all your money. Of course, the Lord is not going to take your money and put it in his own coffers. It is the gesture, your desire to give him all you have that keeps your money safe, and you need only to wait until He shows you what to do with it. You are the banker, the cashier, and God is the owner of your money; He will advise you how to use it so that it will never be lost, for it belongs to him.

Many rich people lose all their money or invest it badly because they have not dedicated it to God; God is the only one who could have advised them how to use it to do good.*

* Related reading: *'Walk While You Have the Light'*, Izvor No. 244, Chap. 13.

2 December

In their desire to be free, human beings have turned away from the Source and accepted a life of slavery and falsehood. And to justify their aberrations, they claim that 'there is no accounting for taste'.* In other words, everyone has their own form of folly and they must be allowed to indulge in the warped behaviour their folly suggests to them.

No, there is a standard for tastes: what is truly good and beautiful is good and beautiful for everyone. You must always choose what is pure, luminous and divine – the range is infinite and you are free to make your own choice. The universe is inhabited by a multitude of angels and archangels, and no one will ask you why you have chosen one angel rather than another – and you are free to be with that angel just as much as you please. It is only if you have chosen a demon that you will be blamed.

* Related reading: *The Laughter of a Sage,* Izvor No. 243, Chap. 10.

3 December

Everything we do, both on the physical and psychic planes, continuously exposes us to impurities. When we eat, drink and breathe, but also when we look or listen, when we associate with certain people or linger in a certain atmosphere, we absorb impure particles and currents that weigh us down and obscure our inner light. For the good of your physical body, you should therefore try to make sure that what you eat and drink is good for your health, and that the air you breathe is clean. For the good of your psychic bodies, you must entertain only thoughts and feelings that are pure.

But there are also some exercises you can do. For instance, several times a day you can imagine that you are as transparent as a crystal. When I say 'imagine' I mean that you must really identify with a crystal, with its transparency, until you begin to feel celestial currents flowing through you, just as light flows through a prism and is refracted into seven colours.*

* Related reading: *Toward a Solar Civilization,* Izvor No. 201, Chap. 7.

4 December

Many serious misunderstandings would be avoided if disciples knew both what they are and are not entitled to expect from their Master. For the road to perfection is infinite and however exalted their Master may be, he is not perfect. Whatever his disciples may think of him, he knows very well that he is far from having attained absolute perfection. Absolute perfection belongs to God alone. This is why disciples who truly love their Master must entertain only the purest and most luminous thoughts and feelings towards him. In this way, not only do they make his work easier but they themselves benefit too, by making it possible for their Master to help them even more.*

* Related reading: *Life with the Master Peter Deunov. Autobiographical Reflections 2.*

5 December

Many people, as long as they are immersed in the atmosphere of a spiritual community, are clearly conscious of being on the right path. They have a clearer perception of the meaning of life; they make efforts to improve themselves, to become wiser, more patient and more in control of themselves.

But once they are back in their usual surroundings and start to socialize again, they soon forget everything they have learned and understood here, and revert to their old habits and attitudes. They even feel a little ashamed of having lived wisely. Why is this? Why does their consciousness change in this way? Because in fact, they had yet to really study or understand things properly. Someone who is truly enlightened will not lose their light even if they associate with the worst deviants or the worst kind of criminals. When wisdom begins to seem stupid, it means that we have abandoned it.*

* Related reading: *A Philosophy of Universality,* Izvor No. 206, Chap. 9.

6 December

Chemists study the constitution and properties of different substances and the conditions (temperature, proportions, etc.) that make it possible to transform them. Very good! But what use is all that to humans if they fail to understand that the same laws apply in their inner lives? That is the trouble; they do not know this. They think that however they go about it, whatever the circumstances, whatever the elements (thoughts, feelings and desires) they introduce into themselves, they will still get what they want.

No, thoughts, feelings and desires are like chemical substances and their properties are just as diverse, so when you bring them together and combine them, the results will also be extremely varied. The laws are the same in the physical and psychic worlds, and it is more important for our inner balance and growth to know the laws of psychic chemistry; otherwise we run the risk of poisoning or burning ourselves, or of blowing everything up.*

* Related reading: *Youth: Creators of the Future,* Izvor No. 233, Chap. 6.

The main thing that prevents people from making progress is their tendency to think that they know it all, that they are as good as they need to be – until of course they experience some mishap. Then the veil falls from their eyes and they realize that they do not know very much after all. At this point, there is at least some hope for them!

One of the best ways of continually moving forward is to compare ourselves with those who have surpassed us, for this gives us an incentive to go further. As long as we compare ourselves with mediocre or bad people, we can say that we are a little more advanced, a little better than they are and rest on our laurels. Why try to be better? We are good enough! So many people cease to evolve simply because they fail to compare themselves with and model themselves on those who are more advanced.*

* Related reading: *Youth: Creators of the Future,* Izvor No. 233, Chap. 13.

8 December

*P*arents and educators often try to impose on young people moral qualities that they themselves do not possess and for which they are unable to set an example. Then they are surprised when their charges refuse to obey or respect them – which is only normal. The life of a true educator must exemplify the qualities and virtues they want to teach to others; they must emanate something contagious, stimulating and irresistible!

A true poet or musician inspires others to become poets or musicians. Someone who is truly a bearer of love opens the hearts of all those around them. A bold and brave general will give his soldiers the courage to launch an attack and carry it through to victory. Imagine a cowardly, timid officer shouting, 'Charge!' in a weak, trembling voice – no one would follow him! Educators say, 'You must be kind, you must be honest, you must be this or that...' while they themselves are none of these things. How can you expect the younger generation to do what they say?*

* Related reading: *The Splendour of Tiphareth – The Yoga of the Sun,* Complete Works, Vol. 10, Chap. 20.

9 December

*M*usic speaks to us of our celestial heritage. From the dawn of time, the language of music has resounded through the cosmos. It is through music that God manifests His love and beauty.

From the initiatic point of view, music supposes a knowledge of the order of the world and of all things, the science of the harmonic relationships in the entire universe, from the microcosm to the macrocosm. Those who transgress the immutable principles on which music rests are lost. Music acts upon our subtle bodies so that we are able once again to be in touch with our heavenly homeland.

10 December

There are more and more knowledgeable, cultured people in the world today, and the sum of knowledge is continually growing in every field. This begs the question as to why, despite all this progress, humanity itself is not improving. On the contrary – the number of delinquents, criminals and mentally ill is even growing. The answer is in fact quite simple: in spite of their learning, educated people's lives continue to be just as chaotic, corrupt and senseless as the lives of the ignorant. More so in fact because their education gives them an even greater scope. The knowledge they acquire remains purely intellectual, theoretical; they never try to integrate it into themselves, to make it penetrate all their cells and become part of their flesh and blood.

The only knowledge that human beings truly lack is the ability to use their knowledge to transform themselves, to spiritualize and illuminate their whole being. Yes, there are too many well-informed people in the world and not enough who are ready to work at their own improvement.*

* Related reading: *Man's Psychic Life: Elements and Structures,* Izvor No. 222, Chap. 8

11 December

*M*ost people when you tell them what they should do to find inner balance, harmony, peace and light, are not against it, but they think that they should first 'experience life for themselves' by tasting all the pleasures and all the dangers it has to offer. Poor wretches! How can they believe that having wasted all their physical and psychic energies in this way they will be in a fit state to do any real inner work? The only thing they will still be able to do will be to read a few books from which they will then quote, 'Moses said... Buddha said... Jesus said...' And it will obviously be impossible for them to put any of these great Masters' precepts into practice.

Well, my advice to you is to do just the opposite: live your lives according to the teaching of the great Masters and stick to quotations for the rest. You can learn all you need to know about human passions by reading the world's literature; it is not necessary to indulge in all kinds of costly experiments. Yes, for there is one kind of life that it is better to live and another kind about which you only need to make a few quotations!*

* Related reading: *Youth: Creators of the Future,* Izvor No. 233, Chap. 5.

12 December

*H*uman beings will never get along or achieve unity* unless their understanding and their attitudes are dictated by a higher point of view. As long as they continue to be ruled by their instincts and appetites, they will never understand each other.

In order to begin to get along, we must enter the realm of feelings, for friendship, affinity and empathy help to draw people together. However, true unity will not be found in the realm of feelings because even there, human beings are often guided by self-interest and the desire for pleasure. You have to go higher, much higher, to the world of wisdom and reason, which is the world of principles. Truth becomes so self-evident on that level that everyone is obliged to see things in the same way.

* Related reading: *Sexual Force or the Winged Dragon,* Izvor No. 205, Chap. 10.

13 December

*B*reathing means not only to take in and expel air, but also to take in and expel light. You must practise this: as you breathe in think that you are drawing in light, and as you breathe out think that you are projecting that light into yourself, into all your cells and all your organs. Then breathe in and breathe out again, and yet again. You will soon see the benefits of this exercise as you begin to feel relaxed and peaceful.

Once you have drawn light into yourself, that you have breathed it in, you can imagine that you are breathing it out to the whole world. Of course, you cannot do this until you have practised the first form of the exercise for a long time and replaced a great many of the sombre, sickly particles of your being with particles of light. You must wait until you sense that your work of transformation and purification has been successful before you can start giving others the light you have received. This work with light is symbolized by the Hebrew letter Aleph א. Aleph is the initiate who receives celestial light, divine life so as to give it to human beings.*

* Related reading: *Harmony and Health,* Izvor No. 225, Chap. 6.

14 December

*H*uman beings are told that they must always be objective; that subjectivity is a dangerous tendency that they should try to get rid of because only what is objective is scientific and real. This only shows that people have never understood the meaning of these two words 'objective' and 'subjective'.

The objective world is composed of material elements that can be examined, measured and weighed, because being material, they are always the same and can be observed in the same way by everybody. The subjective world on the other hand represents life, the emotions, consciousness and the spirit. Nobody wants to study the subjective world because it is variable. They say that no two people can have the same perception of it and therefore that it cannot be grasped, measured or classified. Well, this is a mistake, for if the subjective world is perpetually changing, it is because it is alive, and this means that when you are in touch with it, you are in touch with life.*

---

* Related reading: *Truth, Fruit of Wisdom and Love,* Izvor No. 234, Chap. 11.

15 December

When children break something that belongs to their neighbour or steal their apples, the neighbour comes and complains to the parents, and claims damages from them. And if the parents refuse to pay, they are taken to court. Well, exactly the same process takes place within us. If we allow ourselves to emit negative thoughts and feelings, they are like naughty children who rampage through the invisible world breaking things and doing all kinds of damage. You will say that you cannot be held responsible for your thoughts and feelings because they cannot be controlled. Well, think again. You are responsible for your thoughts and feelings just as you are responsible for your acts.

Nowhere is it written in Initiatic Science that people must be excused for not controlling their thoughts and feelings. On the contrary, for your thoughts and feelings are living, active entities and you have the power to educate them. Human law judges you according to your acts, that is true; but in initiatic teaching, you must learn that divine law judges you also on your thoughts and feelings.

16 December

Some theologians present grace as an arbitrary and inexplicable manifestation of the Deity; nobody knows why grace is given to some people and not to others. It has nothing to do with their conduct or actions, and it is useless to try and understand; that is just the way it is. Presented this way, grace is incompatible with justice and we may wonder if there really is such a thing as divine justice. There is not much to be said for human justice, so if God too is unjust...

No, this is a very bad interpretation of something that is really quite easy to understand. Let me illustrate it. Suppose you are in the process of building a house: the walls are up, but you suddenly realize that you do not have enough money to finish it, so you go to the bank and apply for a loan. If you have sufficient capital, the bank will agree to lend you a certain amount. Does it lend money to everyone? No, but if you already have some capital – some land or assets – it will lend you what you need. In the same way, grace is not given to everybody, only to those who have already prepared themselves, who have already built something and have some capital. Grace says, 'That person is a good worker; they pray and meditate; I will give them what they need to complete the temple they are building.' So, grace is something more than justice, but it nevertheless obeys a form of justice.*

17 December

Many people think that it is a sign of superiority to criticize others and point out their failings; it shows that they are lucid and perceptive. That may well be true, but what they do not know is that their habit of criticizing others and pointing out their faults and failings makes them poorer themselves. When you constantly dwell on people's dishonesty or stupidity, it is as though you were feeding on filth, and something within you begins to degenerate.

If you want to know why Initiates are so rich, let me tell you that it is because they pay attention only to what is most beautiful in human beings: their soul and their spirit. They want to give people's souls and spirits a chance to manifest themselves. This is the key to the wealth of the Initiates. Even though they are aware of the errors and crimes of human beings, they continue to focus on what is best in them. In this way, they help them and enrich themselves as well.

18 December

*S*top chasing after love and you will see that love will chase after you. Even if you want to get rid of it you will not succeed; if you drive it out of the door it will come back in through the window. Yes, as soon as you stop looking for love it comes to you. But the more you chase after it the farther it flees. It is like running after your own shadow: it is always ahead of you, you can never catch up with it. Looking for love from other people is like running after your shadow. So stop looking for it and it will always be there, smiling at you and gazing on you kindly.

You cannot get away from the fact that when you look for love from others, you are concentrating on something outside yourself and you lose the love within you. So instead of looking for love, draw it out from yourself and give it to others and then it will always be within you.*

* Related reading: *New Light on the Gospels,* Izvor No. 217, Chap. 4.

19 December

What will happen if you say to yourself, 'I have made up my mind: I am going to do what is right and help others. I do not care if there is nothing in it for me or if I am not rewarded'? The result will be that you will grow in kindness, patience, generosity and selflessness. Not only will you sense that you are fulfilling yourself, but one day, because of your radiance, you will be appreciated and loved by all.*

A good thought or a good feeling never fails to have an effect, for everything is recorded and leaves a trace. Of course, you must not expect people around you to notice all the goodness in your mind and your heart right away. But you can be sure that one day, all the useful, constructive work you have done by choosing the right path will bring you every blessing. This law is absolute.

* Related reading: *Youth: Creators of the Future,* Izvor No. 233, Chap. 5.

20 December

*T*he only way to master your instinctive impulses is to have a love for a high ideal. And what is a high ideal?* It is a longing for beauty, the spiritual beauty that is purity, light and harmony. When you contemplate this beauty, you naturally and spontaneously turn away from all that is unhealthy, dark and chaotic. Your love of beauty is a protection; it is like a garment that you want to keep clean.

What do you do when you are wearing beautiful clothes that you particularly like? You do not engage in activities in which you would run the risk of tearing or soiling them. You instinctively pay attention to your gestures and look where you sit. Well, in the same way, if you make up your mind to develop your taste for the world of beauty and try to draw closer to it, you will feel as though a subtle garment were gradually being woven around you, and in wanting to protect it, you will be protecting yourself.

* Related reading: *The High Ideal,* Brochure No. 307.

21 December

When you want to light the fire in a fireplace, first you prepare some paper, then some dry twigs, and last of all some bigger pieces of wood. You strike a match and set fire to the paper; the paper communicates the fire to the twigs and the twigs to the logs. This demonstrates a scientific process that also operates in our inner life. The burning match corresponds to the causal plane, the world of the spirit in which all phenomena take their origin; the match sets light to the paper (the mental plane); the paper communicates the flame to the twigs (the astral plane), which in turn set fire to the logs (the physical plane).*

Everything starts on high in the spiritual world, and moves down from one body to the next until it reaches the physical plane. It is important to understand that no true realization is possible on the physical plane unless you begin your work on the spiritual plane.**

* See note and figure on p. 394 and p. 395.

** Related reading: *The Mysteries of Fire and Water,* Izvor No. 232, Chap. 14.

Love expands consciousness and wisdom illuminates it. A picture that appears on the screen of your consciousness may be large but blurred, or clearly defined but very small. This is because in the first case, you failed to work with wisdom; and in the second case, you failed to work with love. Wisdom and love must both be put to work so that your consciousness may be both vast and enlightened. If so many people have such a narrow field of consciousness, it is because they are not interested in anyone else, they do not love anyone. Their consciousness never extends more than an inch or two from their skull. They repeat, 'Me, me, me.'

On the contrary, the consciousness of those who love expands, it reaches out to meet and revolve around others; it stays close to them, and touches and embraces them. Look at people filled with love – they are never still, they are constantly turning to others and taking an interest in their affairs (to the point of sometimes making a nuisance of themselves!) But a person's consciousness can expand and still not be enlightened: the images of love are blurred; they do not give you a clear indication of what you should do. This is why love is not enough; it needs to be accompanied by wisdom.*

* Related reading: *Man's Psychic Life: Elements and Structures,* Izvor No. 222, Chap. 11.

23 December

Even when you feel most deeply discouraged, you must remember that discouragement itself contains elements which, if you know how to grasp and use them properly, will help you to take heart again. For discouragement is a state that possesses tremendous forces. The proof? If discouragement is able to demolish a kingdom – yourself, in spite of all the wealth and potential contained in your physical body, your heart, mind, soul and spirit – it means that it is very powerful indeed. Why not try to take hold of this power and turn it in a positive direction?

Human beings are not aware of all the possibilities that lie within them. Even when they think that they are completely exhausted and at the end of their tether, they still have tremendous inner resources that can help them to get back on their feet and continue on their way.*

* Related reading: *The Seeds of Happiness,* Izvor No. 231, Chap. 9.

24 December

Each one of you must follow the rites of your own religion as much as you wish. We have no desire to impose our convictions on anyone; we want you all to be free to act in harmony with your consciousness and your understanding. In the Brotherhood, we spend the great religious feast days such as Christmas and Easter as simply as all the other days of the year: we pray, meditate and sing together. And even though we may give special thought to the birth, the death or the resurrection of Christ, we have no special ceremony.

Catholics and Protestants, Hindus and Muslims do not all hold the same beliefs or practise the same rites, but is that a reason for them to fight each other? No. It is contrary to wisdom to poison other people's lives just because you follow the teachings of one particular religious founder. Instead of continually stirring up unrest and strife, people should be brotherly, and embrace and help each other. In doing so, they will show that they are followers of true religion.*

* Related reading: *A Philosophy of Universality,* Izvor No. 206, Chap. 5.

25 December

The task of disciples is to build within themselves the spiritual body that will enable them to be born a second time. They already possess the idea: the kingdom of God and His righteousness, perfection, celestial harmony. All they need to do now is to gather the materials to construct the building.

Actually, once the idea is there, the materials will come by themselves. When you have an idea, a blueprint, and you expose it, it draws all the necessary elements from the cosmos, which come and arrange themselves according to the overall design. Your own work is to keep the plan firmly fixed in your heart and soul. This is how your spiritual body – the body of glory, the body of Christ – gradually takes shape within you. What is known as the second birth is the formation of this luminous body, which enables human beings to live and act on the spiritual plane.*

* Related reading: *Christmas and Easter in the Initiatic Tradition,* Izvor No. 209, Chap. 2.

26 December

It is by linking ourselves to the heavenly Source that our own source can begin to spring forth. It must flow first of all in our hearts, through love. Whatever happens, whatever the bitter experiences, disappointments or trials, we must always keep the spring of love open within us for this is how the heart is purified.

In our intellect, the divine Source flows down as light.* Thanks to this light, we can avoid pitfalls and obstacles; we can see the path ahead of us and follow it confidently.

When the divine Source penetrates our soul, it opens it out to the far reaches of the universe. We lose ourselves in immensity; we bear all creatures within us; we embrace the whole world.

And when at last we have succeeded in making the divine Source flow in our heart, intellect and soul, it merges with the primordial Source, which is our spirit, which is God Himself. In this way, we become powerful with the power of God.

* Related reading: *Life with the Master Peter Deunov. Autobiographical Reflections 2.*

27 December

You say that among the people you see around you, there are no examples of morality and spiritual elevation for you to follow. Are you sure of that? Well, even if you are right, let me tell you that it is not absolutely necessary to meet living examples on the physical plane; books can also be useful. Yes, there are plenty of books that tell of the life and work of the sages, saints, Initiates and great Masters of the past. Read them to learn what kind of people they were and what they did, and then compare this to what you are and what you have accomplished.

I will even go so far as to say that it is not enough to compare yourself to human beings, however exalted. You must also compare yourself to the stars, to the immensity of the universe, to God Himself. This is the best way to become conscious of how small and inadequate we are, not in order to be overwhelmed, but in order to awaken within us the impulse to leap forward and surmount every obstacle.*

* Related reading: Youth: *Creators of the Future,* Izvor No. 233, Chap. 13.

28 December

*T*he power of Initiates lies in their ability to infuse their words with the abundant, intense, pure matter of their own aura. A word is a vehicle for a force, and the more fully it is impregnated with the creative element of light, the more potent will be its effect.

The ability to pronounce powerful words of magic is not given to just anyone. But an Initiate can utter such words without raising their voice, without a gesture, and the inner power of their aura will be enough to command the forces of nature and draw higher beings to their side. The world was not created by the spoken word but by the Divine Word, the Logos. Words are the instruments with which the Logos accomplishes the work of creation. The Logos is the original element set in motion by God, and it is by means of the spoken word that the Logos is able to manifest itself.*

* Related reading: *The Book of Divine Magic,* Izvor No. 226, Chap. 4.

29 December

We sometimes hear people complaining 'I am all alone, I have no family.' What! No family? They have an immense family, but their consciousness is so narrow and clouded that they do not feel it. There are millions of people in the world in this situation. They feel as though they were alone, and yet...!

You at least can work to expand your consciousness. You must realize that even if you no longer had a father or mother or brothers or sisters or any blood relation, you would still have no reason to believe that you were alone. You must know and feel that you are all brothers and sisters, all sons and daughters of the same Father, the Cosmic Spirit, and of the same Mother, Universal Nature, and that you will never again be abandoned or miserable.*

* Related reading: *Youth: Creators of the Future,* Izvor No. 233, Chap. 20.

30 December

*T*he earth is predestined to become a reflection of heaven. At the moment, this is not yet the case. The earth – that is to say the world of humans – does not vibrate in harmony, in tune with heaven. When human beings become conscious of the task for which they have incarnated, they will begin to work on the earth, on 'their' earth, which is to say themselves. They will make their whole being vibrate in unison with the divine world in order to reflect the order, beauty and light that are on high.

And as the state of the planet on which we live is tied to the degree of humanity's evolution, it too will change; it too will become subtle, vibrant and luminous, and will produce other fruits and other plants and flowers. Everything will change on account of the lives of human beings, simply because they will have come to understand the work they need to do on themselves in order to transform themselves.*

* Related reading: *Love Greater Than Faith,* Izvor No. 239, Chap. 7.

31 December

In certain traditions, the universe is represented as a mountain whose summit is God's inaccessible, inviolate dwelling place. The Greek gods dwelt on the top of Mount Olympus; Moses spoke to God on Mount Sinai, and so forth. Initiates have always used the symbol of the peak or summit, even in countries where there were no real mountains.

The quest for the summit is the most important, most meaningful endeavour a human being can undertake. It means that we know that the powers and virtues bestowed on us by the Creator can lead us to heights far beyond any earthly achievements. In the Cabbalah, the Sephirotic Tree of Life* can be seen as a mountain whose summit is the sephirah *Kether*: omnipotence, omniscience and divine love. To reach this summit, great qualities of tenacity, willpower, stability, intelligence and daring are needed, and above all an irresistible yearning for the light and purity represented by all the other sephiroth.**

* See note and figure on p. 396-399.

** Related reading: *Sunrise Meditations,* Brochure No. 323, Chap. 24.

The Night of Wesak

*E*ach year, in the Himalayas, during the night of the full moon in May, the ceremony of Wesak takes place.*

The full moon in May is doubly under the influence of Taurus: the sun has been in this sign since 21 April, and the moon is also exalted in this sign.** Taurus represents prolific nature, fertility and abundance, emphasized further by the fact that it is the home of Venus, the planet of creation. So the full moon in May offers the best conditions for working with the forces of nature to attract heaven's blessings for the harvest and livestock, but also for human beings. For, if humans know how to attract the beneficial effects circulating through the cosmos at this time, they too can benefit from them, not only on the physical plane but also on the spiritual plane. This is why, by means of meditations, prayers, chants and magical invocations, initiates seek to create lines of force in space that will attract energies, which they send to all beings who are vigilant, awakened and capable of participating at this event.

* Wesak is the festival of the Buddha. In Tibet, it is celebrated in the valley of Wesak.

** Some years, when the sun is in Taurus, the full moon takes place in April.

There are places on earth that are more favourable than others for this cosmic work. The site where the ceremony of Wesak takes place is the most powerful of all. Some initiates go there physically, others by astral projection. But it is possible for everyone, including you, to take part in thought. During this night, you must not keep any metal object on you, since metal is not a good conductor of the waves of energy that come down from spiritual regions. But the only truly essential condition for being admitted to this festival is harmony. So be careful not to hold onto any negative thought or feeling towards others, and find the right inner attitude that will allow you to receive the blessings that the initiates send to the children of God on this night.

INDEX

A

Academic knowledge – useful but superficial, 16 Sept.

Act of lovemaking – it should improve, uplift and strengthen your partner, 23 Feb.

Adam Kadmon – the body of the universe of which human beings are a part, 3 Feb.

Advancing – by imitating those who surpass us, 14 March

Alchemy – true alchemy is spiritual alchemy, 23 April

Alcohol and drugs – a harmful illusion of freedom, 28 Oct.

Aquarius bring the ideas of brotherhood and universality, 31 Jan.

Artists must make the spirit descend into matter, 23 Oct.

Asserting oneself – by means of light, love and gentleness, 8 May

Aura – its quality depends on the way we live, 17 March

B

Bad thoughts and feelings – how to remain above them, 22 Sept.

Balance – there is no such thing as absolute equilibrium, 20 Feb.

Beauty – more to do with kindness than intelligence, 20 July

Black Madonna – the transmutation of matter, 13 Nov.

Breaking the law – adding debts to be paid, 16 July

Breath – the beginning and the end of life, 11 April

Breathing – think of light as you breathe in and project it as you breathe out, 13 Dec.

Brotherhood – under the protection of the entities of the sun, 27 Aug.

Bureau of Weights and Measures – universal standards, 9 Nov.

C

Candle – through it, we make contact with the four elements, 18 Nov.

Cells – they revolt if the head is no longer in charge, 19 March

Chastity – seek love on the spiritual plane, 3 Aug.

Children
- parents must teach them the meaning of effort, 14 Oct.
- they possess great sensitivity when they are very young, 7 Sept.

Christmas – forming a spiritual body in order to be born a second time, 25 Dec.

Collective life – thinking of others, of all of humankind, 30 July

Communion – establishing contact with the vital forces of nature, 28 Jan.

Concentrate on all that is luminous, 25 April

Consciousness
- attained by beings who become collective, universal, 18 April
- love expands it and wisdom illuminates it, 22 Dec.

Consciousness and subconscious – image of the lotus, 19 Aug.

Consideration – it reduces or heightens the effectiveness of things, 20 June

Constraints – they strengthen our will, 12 May

Conventional science – one day it will confirm Initiatic Science, 25 March

Cosmic Intelligence – it increases one's clarity of mind, 16 April

Cosmic Love – it gives us time to mend our ways, 23 Sept.

Cosmic Spirit – it has a different perspective from that of the earth, 26 Oct.

Creation – acknowledging that it has a Creator, 27 April

Criticizing others – it makes you poorer, 17 Dec.

Curiosity – beware of traps, 15 April

D

Daath – the sephirah that possesses all the memory of the world, 19 Oct.

Decisions – try to foresee what they might lead to, 1 Aug.

Desires and Projects – never neglect the moral aspect, 25 July

Destiny – we are free to do good or evil, 8 Sept.

Development – human beings must grow and develop on every plane, 6 March

Devil – he cannot enter without permission, 17 May

Devil's role – getting human beings who break the laws to behave, 11 Aug.

Difficulties

- do not look gloomy; try to shine instead, 15 Feb.

- rough edges that allow us to climb, 10 Aug.

- we must not try to escape them, but try to solve them, 31 Aug.

Disciple

- it is never too late to devote oneself to a sublime ideal, 21 Oct.

- verify the origin of all your motives, 15 Jan.

Disciples – like orchards that luminous spirits come to visit, 4 June

Discouragement

- renew your courage when you encounter difficulties, 11 Jan.

- turn it in a positive direction, 23 Dec.

Divine Laws – and the laws of nature, 5 Nov.

Divine Love – project it outward to all of creation, 12 Aug.

E

Earth – and human beings will one day become a reflection of heaven, 30 Dec.

Eating – do so in a state of harmony and meditation, 2 Oct.

Echo – the beneficial or harmful waves are sent back, 12 July

Economy

- it begins with wisdom and moderation, 29 June
- true economy is to be careful and pay attention, 13 Sept.

Educators – focus on the divine spark in each child, 12 Feb.

Efforts – they keep us strong and intelligent, 7 July

Electricity – the type of heating that corresponds symbolically to Initiates, 21 March

Emanations – they may contain curative or toxic elements, 28 Nov.

Emanations of a spiritual being – beneficial to all creatures, 1 Sept.

Enlightened – when we are truly enlightened, we stay on the right path, 5 Dec.

Equilibrium – work with both wisdom and love, 16 June

Esoteric Science – begin by studying it in daily life, 26 Feb.

Evil – the Initiates and spiritual Masters know how to use it, 26 Aug.

Evolution – a struggle against the weight and obscurity of our being, 4 Jan.

Evolving – comparing ourselves to those who have surpassed us, 7 Dec.

Excesses – they can cause irreparable losses, 5 March

Exercises with light – there is nothing more potent, 28 April

Expressive face – the only thing that can satisfy a husband or a wife, 25 Nov.

External conditions – a Master also sees the inner riches, 3 Oct.

F

Fairy tale about the princess and the dragon – its meaning, 31 March

Faith – it opens a door through which grace can enter, 29 April

Faults – do not dwell on other people's faults, 17 April

Fear – the only legitimate fear is the fear of breaking the divine laws, 30 Nov.

Feet – connected to the brain and the solar plexus, 3 July

Fire – the spiritual fire of divine love transforms human beings, 5 Jan.

Food – impart harmonious vibrations to it, 4 Sept.

Four Elements
- their correspondences in life, 16 March
- they respect only the image of God, 18 March

Four-Part Singing – correspondence with a violin, 17 Aug.

Freedom
- achieving it through your own efforts, 28 Aug.
- for those who are governed by the spirit, by light, 4 Oct.
- we must first pay our debts and wipe out our karma, 31 May

Friendship – true friends tell each other the truth, 11 Nov.

Friendship and love – intellectual compatibility is required, 30 May

Fullness and Emptiness – they work together in the universe, 26 Nov.

Future
- creating a divine future by means of thought, 15 May
- determined by our choice of light or darkness, 6 July

G

Generosity – it requires knowledge of the art of saving, 4 July

Gestures – touch and move objects lovingly, 7 Oct.

Giving Thanks – the words "thank you" ease all tension, 14 June

God created us in His image and likeness, 24 Sept.

God's Name – Yod He Vav He, the four principles within man, 24 Oct.

Going Without – depriving oneself a little in order to reap an abundant harvest, 12 Sept.

Good – it is as powerful as evil, 5 Sept.

Goodness

- sooner or later, it will bring you every blessing, 19 Dec.
- the fruits that human beings must bear, 29 Oct.

Grace – it is given to those who have some capital, 16 Dec.

Grain of Wheat – its adventures reflect our evolution, 25 Sept.

H

Happiness

- look for it in the higher regions, 20 May
- look for the elements that nourish it, 28 March
- seeking it is a form of the quest for God, 14 Nov.
- the result of love, not of knowledge, 8 Aug.
- true happiness lies in the efforts we make, 9 March

Hardship – a last resort to make human beings think, 4 Aug.

Harmony

- find it without tasting all of life's pleasures, 11 Dec.
- seek it in order to become a beneficent force, 7 Jan.

Head – a Master can tell a person's nature from the structure of their head, 23 May

Health – taking only what we need, 12 March

Heart – do not give it away, rather give your finest sentiments, 11 Feb.

Heart and intellect – they must work together, 21 Sept.

Heart, intellect and will – unite these three powers, 19 May

Heaven – never abandon it, 15 July

Heaven and Earth – their exchanges produce life, 18 Oct.

Heavenly hierarchy – knowledge of it is indispensable, 1 July

Heavenly Source – by linking ourselves to it, our own source can spring forth, 26 Dec.

Helping others – useful to them and to oneself, 24 Nov.

High Ideal

- a magical element that brings harmony, 17 June
- longing for the spiritual beauty that protects us, 20 Dec.

Higher Self – it is in the sun; establishing a bond with it, 27 May

Holy Spirit – its coming is the most sublime experience, 28 May

Homeopathic doses – first, they act on our subtle bodies, 1 Feb.

Human Beings need to be roused, stimulated and shaken up, 25 Oct.

Human Body – it could live much longer, 6 May

Human Concerns – insignificant to Cosmic Intelligence, 1 June

Human Spirit – it is not bound by material conditions, 10 April

I

Idea – a luminous being, a living entity that visits you, 6 Jan.

Ideal – work for universal brotherhood, 27 Sept.

Identification – attuning ourselves to the same wavelength, 21 Jan.

Identification or fusion – something only the spirit can do, 3 Sept.

Incarnation – the spirits of light are also subject to heredity, 13 June

Inertia of the mind and heart – it takes willpower to overcome it, 4 Feb.

Inertia – react, get moving again by means of thought, 23 Aug.

Initiates – like a tree, they give away their fruit, 25 Jan.

Initiates – their legacy is invaluable to us, 27 Feb.

Initiatic Science – put the truths into practice, 21 May

Initiations – they all teach about fusion with God, 27 June

Inner Face – that of our soul, which is different from our physical face, 14 Aug.

Inner Life

- become conscious of its wealth, 10 July

- developing it is like lighting a fire, 21 Dec.

Inner Life and chemistry – governed by the same laws, 6 Dec.

Inner Peace – free yourself by making amends for your mistakes, 27 July

Instincts – confront them with luminous powers, 14 April

Intellect – it often works against moral values, 6 Feb.

Intelligence – do not judge or criticize others, 8 Nov.

Invisible things – without realizing it, everyone believes in invisible things, 28 June

Isis Unveiled – contemplating her is the culmination of the Initiate's journey, 9 Oct.

J

Joy – experience it without going to extremes, 19 Jan.

Joy – the greatest joy comes from being one with the Creator, 29 May

Joy and Suffering – they depend on our vibrations, 13 April

Justice – the law of love will always transcend justice, 22 May

K

Karma – it should not be an excuse for doing nothing to help others, 8 July

Kingdom – it awaits us following an apprenticeship, 23 July

Kingdom of God

- a great number of people must want it, 16 May

- those who serve it are rewarded, 23 Jan.

Kingdom of God

- by wishing for it, we elevate ourselves and help humanity, 22 Nov.
- work for this ideal, 9 May

Knowledge – use it to spiritualize and illuminate your whole being, 10 Dec.

L

Lack – realizing that we are extremely rich, 14 Sept.

Letter M – the expression of a whole science, 2 May

Life

- like a journey of discovery within ourselves too, 10 Jan.
- treasure it in order to obtain everything the soul and spirit desire, 22 Jan.

Life and death – always help to maintain life, 17 Sept.

Life is in our image – beautiful when we are beautiful, 9 Aug.

Light

- let it be your inner yardstick, 13 Jan.
- liquid gold on the spiritual plane, 10 Sept.
- protecting ourselves against the spirits of darkness, 17 Nov.
- the speed of our thoughts and spirit is even faster, 3 April

Likes and Dislikes – the importance of reasoning, 20 Sept.

Living – a pure life attracts marvellous beings, 29 March

Logos, the Word – it is this that gives your words their potency, 26 Jan.

Looks – they must bring harmony, 25 Feb.

The **Lord** does not need to be defended, 26 June

Love

- always the same force but with many degrees, 26 March
- as soon as you stop looking for it, love comes to you, 18 Dec.
- disseminated everywhere, in the whole of creation, 25 May

Love

- harmonizes everything within you and around you, 16 Oct.
- it must make those you love grow, 17 Jan.
- send it to the sublime entities, 15 Oct.
- what to do if the other person turns their back on the light, 29 Nov.
- why people should keep a little distance between them, 24 April
- without realizing it, we are immersed in it, 11 March
- without expecting to be loved back – you will be free, 14 Feb.

Lower Nature – in danger of making humankind disappear, 10 June

Luminous Spirits – get them to visit you by working to purify yourself, 13 May

M

Magic

- a look, a gesture... everything is magic, 4 Nov.
- adding a quality to beings and things, 20 Nov.

Magic is based on the gestures of everyday life, 13 Feb.

Magic Wand – a live connection between earth and heaven, 3 June

Master

- consider him like an envoy from heaven, 24 Feb.
- he makes a great sacrifice to take care of human beings, 9 Feb.
- nourishes his disciples with his light, 24 Aug.
- his face speaks of the divine world, 29 Jan.
- send him pure thoughts and feelings, 4 Dec.

The **Master and Life** – together they educate human beings, 20 Oct.

Matter – it satisfies only our physical needs, 18 Aug.

Matter and Spirit – achieving the fusion of both, 12 Oct.

Maya – the often-deceptive appearance of things, 21 April

Meaning of Life – only the divine world can give it to us, 30 Aug.

Meditate to commune with God through your higher soul, 3 Jan.

Meditating – attracting celestial light and sending it out to the whole world, 9 June

Meditating – do not concentrate abruptly, 30 June

Meditation – detaching ourselves from our restrictive lower self, 30 Sept.

Mercury – the combination of the Sun, the Moon and the Earth, 8 April

Miracles – they are not supernatural; they obey the laws of the spirit, 6 Aug.

Mission – reconciling our inner life and our life in the world, 16 Feb.

Moments of silence – to recover your inner peace and balance, 15 March

Money – dedicate everything to the Lord, even your money, 1 Dec.

Highest **Moral Law** – love your enemies, 26 July

Moral Qualities – to face life's difficulties, 2 Aug.

Morality – differences between the laws of nature and the laws of humans, 19 June

Mountain tops – they pick up and distribute the forces of the cosmos, 12 April

Mountains

- focus on their symbolic, living aspect, 4 March

- inhabited by very luminous and powerful entities, 15 Aug.

Moving up in Rank – internally so as to be obeyed by our cells, 5 June

Music – it manifests the love and beauty of God, 9 Dec.

N

Name

- it must express the quintessence of the being who bears it, 18 Feb.
- saying an entity's name to call on their help, 7 March

Nature

- get into the habit of watching and listening to the four elements, 2 July
- like Nature, humans must apportion heat and moisture, 31 Oct.

Negative states – learn to fly away by means of thought, 1 Nov.

New Year – clear out your old thoughts, feelings and habits, 1 Jan.

Noise – take care not to disturb others; the benefits, 23 Nov.

Nourishing ourselves – with light for the sake of our brain, 31 July

O

Objectivity and Subjectivity – the two are inextricably linked, 14 July

Occult Powers – prepare and purify yourself in order to obtain them, 10 Feb.

Old Age – it can be the best period of one's life, 3 March

P

Parable of the Prodigal Son – departure and return, 20 Aug.

Perfecting Oneself – always cling to your desire to improve, 30 April

Perseverance – rely on the powers of the spirit, 18 June

Peter Deunov (precept) – "goodness, justice, wisdom, love and truth", 8 June

Physical Appearance – it does not always correspond to one's psyche, 2 Feb.

Physical Body – free yourself from its domination, 13 Oct.

Plants and stones – they have a form of sensitivity, 19 Nov.

Pleasure – using this natural inclination constructively,
6 Nov.

True **Poetry** – awakens a reminiscence of Paradise, 22 Oct.

Poisoning – not only on the physical plane but also on the
psychic plane, 17 July

Pollution – also and foremost in the psychic world, 11 June

Possessions – be content to have just what you need, 7 Nov.

Praise – do not seek it if you want to be able to move forward,
19 Feb.

Prayer

- done correctly, it gives results, 5 Aug.

- it acts upon our psychic bodies and our physical body, 18 Jan.

- it must be expressed in the three worlds, 27 March

- the ability to concentrate and to wish, 21 Feb.

Prayers – address them to the beings who are nearest to
humans, 9 Jan.

Praying

- enter into your secret room and shut the door, 7 Feb.

- imagine a living, radiant centre, 27 Oct.

Problems

- life constantly offers us new problems to solve, 13 July

- set them aside and go on a retreat sometimes, 25 June

Protecting oneself – from negative influences and currents,
13 Aug.

Protection – on the physical plane and on the spiritual plane,
6 June

Psychic shortcomings – they cannot be assuaged by physical
remedies, 13 March

Purity – imagine that you are as transparent as a crystal,
3 Dec.

R

Read about the life and work of the Initiates and the great Masters, 27 Dec.

Reaping what we have sown with our words and deeds, 17 Oct.

Recordings – correct those that are negative, 15 Nov.

Reincarnation – family relationships from a past life, 2 Sept.

Relations – between human beings and the forces of nature, 1 March

Relativity – feeling happy or unhappy, 27 Nov.

Religions

- their concern is to get human beings to turn back to God, 8 Feb.

- they must all be brotherly and help one another, 24 Dec.

Renunciation – its purpose is to obtain something better, 20 Jan.

Resilience – obtained through the practice of virtues, 19 Sept.

Responsibilities – do not choose the easy way out, 16 Nov.

Responsibility – we are responsible for our thoughts and feelings, 15 Dec.

Resurrection – the caterpillar must become a butterfly, 9 April

Riches – by seeking the soul and spirit of others, you will find true riches, 11 July

Riches – one day, our inner and outer riches will match, 28 Feb.

Rising high – to build one's spiritual bodies, 20 April

Running wild – it poses a risk of physical and moral ruin, 10 Nov.

S

Seed or the pit – no part of the fruit is more important, 12 Nov.

Self-Centredness – others avoid that which is closed-off and icy, 5 Oct.

Self-Mastery – to become the ruler of one's kingdom, 10 May

Selfishness – we defend our own interests by thinking of others, 10 March

Sensuality – it prevents us from reaching the heavenly regions, 21 June

Sexual energy – it must further our spiritual growth, 16 Aug.

Sexual force – of the same nature as solar energy, 15 June

Sexuality – instinctive sexuality feeds inferior entities, 3 May

Shepherd – chases away the wolves from within with light, 23 June

Silence – a source of harmony and beauty, 14 May

Silence – it allows the divine Spirit to work upon us, 1 Oct.

Silence and concentration – detaching oneself completely from all one's cares, 1 May

Skin – a language, the reflection of our inner being, 29 Aug.

Solar rays – they give life to beings and objects, 5 July

Solitude – a trial that even Christ had to go through, 24 June

Solitude – it does not exist for those who know how to expand their consciousness, 29 Dec.

Sorrow – force yourself to rise to the level of reason, 28 Sept.

Sphinx – it represents the zodiac and the four elements, 5 Feb.

Spirit – it seeks to manifest itself through matter, 22 July

Spirit – true strength lies within, in the spirit, 25 Aug.

Spiritual Brotherhood – prevents us from doing something foolish, 4 April

Spiritual life – apply simple methods every day, 16 Jan.

Spiritual life – it is never too late to start to develop it, 2 Jan.

Spiritual love – true happiness, 3 Nov.

Spiritual work – no immediately visible results, 2 June

Spiritual work – the difference between it and ordinary work, 27 Jan.

Squaring the circle – matter (the square) vivified by the spirit (the circle), 2 March

Subconscious – rising and preparing oneself before diving in, 30 March

Subjective world – it represents life and the spirit, 14 Dec.

Suffering – know how to accept and understand it, 8 March

Suffering – others always deserve our help when they are suffering, 7 June

Summit – the quest for the summit is the most important undertaking, 31 Dec.

Sun

- a universal language that everyone understands, 11 May

- it teaches us how to become luminous, warm and life giving, 23 March

- radiate light like the sun, the highest possible ideal, 28 July

- storing up its rays in our solar plexus, 12 June

- uniting with it by means of thought raises our vibrations, 5 April

Sunrise – prepare yourself to watch it the evening before, 4 May

T

Talisman – a source of either good or bad influences, 18 Sept.

Tastes – there is a universal standard, 2 Dec.

Thank the Lord in order to take in the light, 11 Oct.

The Lord's Prayer – bringing about heaven on earth, 22 Feb.

The Teaching – it contains everything we need to overcome our sorrows, 26 Sept.

The Teaching – it must become an intrinsic part of you, 7 April

Thought – it allows us to attain perfection, 21 Nov.

Thought – it can find anything in the universe thanks to the law of affinity, 26 May

Thoughts – how to make them become reality more quickly, 5 May

Thoughts – they play a vital role for the future of humankind, 9 Sept.

Thoughts to offer help – like little angels that come to the rescue, 10 Oct.

Thoughts and feelings – at the root of our actions, 1 April

Thoughts and feelings – be aware of the boomerang effect, 15 Sept.

To know, to will, to dare, to keep silent – why we should keep silent, 21 Aug.

Torments – a toxic substance to be transformed, 22 Aug.

Tree – correspondence with a human being, 20 March

Tree – every human being has the ability to blossom just like a tree, 18 May

Tree of Life – the pillars of mercy and severity, 29 Sept.

Trees and human beings – in both, the highest is linked to the lowest, 11 Sept.

Trials – begin by calming yourself and thinking, 26 April

Troubles – flee from the entities chasing us, 19 April

Truth – the sages and Initiates receive it first, 21 July

U

Unhappiness – extricate yourself from this state by turning on your inner lamps, 30 Oct.

Unity – requires a higher, shared point of view, 12 Dec.

Unity – understanding 'strength in unity' internally, 6 Oct.

Universal White Brotherhood – it is the religion of Christ, 12 Jan.

Universe – our whole being is linked to all of creation, 2 April

V

Vibrations – intensify them to project rays of life into the world, 24 May

Vices – rising higher to conquer and transform them, 8 Jan.

Vices – we can take away their power, 8 Oct.

Voice – cultivate and strengthen it by leading a pure life, 14 Jan.

W

Washing oneself – a sacred act that can liberate our soul, 18 July

Water

- a source of life and love, 24 March
- exercise with a glass filled with water, 22 April
- for humans as for water, there are two possible methods of purification, 9 July
- it has powers of absorption and transmission, 7 May

Weaknesses – enrol in the school of strength instead, 2 Nov.

White Magic – the secret is to have the right attitude, 6 Sept.

Willpower – it develops when conditions are difficult, 24 Jan.

Wisdom is like gold that attracts heavenly creatures, 30 Jan.

Women – outer beauty and inner beauty, 7 Aug.

Word of an Initiate – imbued with the light of their aura, 28 Dec.

Work – sublime work entails striving towards the perfection of God, 22 June

Work for a divine idea – it gives you everything, 24 July

Work honestly – one day you will be recognized for what you are, 29 July

Work that is directed towards a divine goal gives meaning to life, 17 Feb.

Working – participating in a celestial enterprise, 19 July

Y

Young people – making them aware of the soul and the spirit, 6 April

Youth – teaching them by setting an example, 8 Dec.

Note: The three fundamental activities which characterize human beings are thinking (by means of the intellect or mind), feeling (by means of the heart), and doing (by means of the physical body). You must not believe that only the physical body is material; the heart and mind are also material instruments, but the matter of which they are made is far subtler than that of the physical body.

HIGHER NATURE

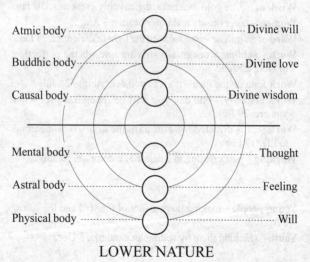

Atmic body ·············· Divine will

Buddhic body ··········· Divine love

Causal body ············· Divine wisdom

Mental body ············· Thought

Astral body ·············· Feeling

Physical body ··········· Will

LOWER NATURE

An age-old esoteric tradition teaches that the support or vehicle of feeling is the astral body, and that of the intellect, the mental body. But this trinity made up of our physical, astral, and mental bodies, constitutes our imperfect human nature, and the three faculties of thought, feeling, and action also exist on a higher level, their vehicles being respectively, the causal, buddhic, and atmic bodies which go to make up our divine self.

In the diagram, the three large concentric circles indicate the links which exist between the lower and the higher bodies. The physical body, which represents strength, will, and power on the material level, is linked to the atmic body, which represents divine power, strength, and will. The astral body, which represents our egotistical, personal feelings and desires, is linked to the buddhic body, which represents divine love. The mental body, which represents our ordinary, self-serving thoughts, is linked to the causal body, which represents divine wisdom.

(Man's Psychic Life: Elements and Structures, Izvor Collection No. 222, chap. 3)

Introduction to the Sephirotic Tree

Jesus said, 'And this is eternal life, that they may know you, the only true God'.

For those who aspire to know the Creator of heaven and earth, to feel his presence, to enter into his infinity and his eternity, it is necessary to have a deep understanding of a system that explains the world. The system that seemed to me to be the best, the most extensive and at the same time the most precise I found in the cabbalistic tradition – the sephirotic Tree, the Tree of Life. Its knowledge offers the deepest, most structured, overall view of what we need to study and work on.

The cabbalists divide the universe into ten regions or ten sephiroth corresponding to the first ten numbers (the word 'sephirah' and its plural 'sephiroth' mean enumeration). Each sephirah is identified by means of five names: the name of God, the name of the sephirah, the name of the archangel at the head of the angelic order, the angelic order itself, and a planet. God directs these ten regions, but under a different name in each one. This is why the Cabbalah gives God ten names, each corresponding to different attributes. God is one, but manifests in a different way in each region.

This Tree of Life is presented as a very simple diagram, but its contents are inexhaustible. For me it is the key that allows the mysteries of creation to be deciphered. It is not meant to teach us astronomy or cosmology, and anyway no one can say exactly what the universe is or how it was created. This Tree represents an explanatory system of the world that is by nature mystical. Through meditation and contemplation and a life of saintliness, the exceptional minds that devised it came to grasp a cosmic reality, and it is essentially their teaching that survives to this day, passed down by tradition and continually taken up and meditated on through the centuries.

A spiritual Master is conscious of the responsibilities he is taking by allowing humans to enter this holy sanctuary, and so when you approach this knowledge you must do so with much humility, respect and reverence. By returning often to this diagram, you will find lights being switched on inside you. You will certainly never manage to explore all its riches, but from Malkuth to Kether this representation of an ideal world will always draw you higher.

TREE OF LIFE

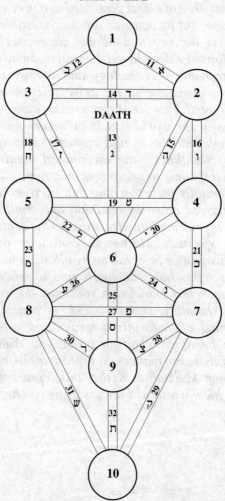

TREE OF LIFE

1 Ehieh
Kether – *Crown*
Metatron
Hayoth haKadesch – *Seraphim*
Rashith haGalgalim – *First Swirlings (Neptune)*
Ψ

3 Jehovah
Binah – *Understanding*
Tzaphkiel
Aralim – *Thrones*
Shabbathai – *Saturn*
♄

2 Yah
Chokmah – *Wisdom*
Raziel
Ophanim – *Cherubim*
Mazloth – *The Zodiac (Uranus)*
♅

5 Elohim Gibor
Geburah – *Severity*
Kamaël
Seraphim – *Powers*
Maadim – *Mars*
♂

4 El
Chesed – *Mercy*
Tzsadkiel
Hashmalim – *Dominations*
Tzedek – *Jupiter*
♃

6 Eloha vaDaath
Tiphareth – *Beauty*
Mikhaël
Malakhim – *Virtues*
Shemesh – *Sun*
☉

8 Elohim Tzebaoth
Hod – *Glory*
Raphaël
Bnei-Elohim – *Archangels*
Kokab – *Mercury*
☿

7 Jehovah Tzebaoth
Netzach – *Victory*
Haniel
Elohim – *Principalities*
Noga – *Venus*
♀

9 Shaddai El Hai
Yesod – *Foundation*
Gabriel
Kerubim – *Angels*
Levana – *Moon*
☽

10 Adonai-Melek
Malkuth – *The Kingdom*
Uriel (Sandalfon)
Ishim – *Beatified Souls*
Olem Ha Yesodoth – *Earth*
♁

Worldwide Editor and Distributor

Editions Prosveta (France)

www.prosveta.fr • www.prosveta.com • contact@prosveta.fr

Tel. +33 4 94 19 33 33

For an updated list, please visit
www.prosveta.fr

English Distributors

AUSTRALIA
Prosveta Australia • prosveta.au@aapt.net.au
CANADA
Prosveta • www.prosveta-canada.com • prosveta@prosveta-canada.com
FRANCE
Editions Prosveta • www.prosveta.fr • international@prosveta.com
IRELAND
Prosveta UK • www.prosveta.co.uk • orders@prosveta.co.uk
LEBANON
Prosveta Liban • www.prosveta-liban.com • prosveta_lb@terra.net.lb
NETHERLANDS
Stichting Prosveta Nederland • www.prosveta.nl • vermeulen@prosveta.nl
NEW ZEALAND
Prosveta New Zealand • www.oma-books.co.nz
johnson.susan34@gmail.com
NORWAY
Prosveta Norden • www.prosveta.no • info@prosveta.no
UNITED KINGDOM
Prosveta UK • www.prosveta.co.uk • orders@prosveta.co.uk
UNITED STATES OF AMERICA
Wellsprings of Life • www.prosveta-usa.com • wellspringsoflife@mail.com
Prosveta Books • www.prosvetabooks.com • prosvetausa@gmail.com

Printed in June 2022
by PRINTCORP

Dépôt légal : juin 2022